Literacy, Vocabulary, and Acculturation

ABOUT THE NATIONAL ASSOCIATION FOR MULTICULTURAL EDUCATION (NAME) SERIES

Editors: Abul Pitre and Ashraf Esmail

Educators in the 21st century face enormous challenges as a result of *No Child Left Behind* and *Race to The Top*. The requirements embedded into these high accountability policies have exacerbated the disparities that exist in schools that serve historically underserved students, particularly students of color. Educators are being tasked with raising test scores and high stakes testing along with prepackaged curriculum are placing educators and students in a psychic prison.

In this compelling series we invite scholars and practitioners to address issues of diversity, equity, and social justice. The series seeks to provide books that will help educators to navigate the terrain of high stakes testing that has resulted in the pedagogy of poverty. Drawing from critical multicultural education the series invites scholars and practitioners who have an interest in critical pedagogy, critical race theory, antiracist education, religious diversity, critical theories in education and social justice to provide practicing educators with knowledge to address the contemporary problems that have wreaked havoc on underserved students. This compelling series particularly speaks to practicing educators who hold positions as *leaders, teachers, counselors, coaches, mentors, paraprofessionals, and others involved with student learning.*

Literacy, Vocabulary, and Acculturation

A Critical Education Triangle for English Language Learners

Edited by
Ashraf Esmail, Abul Pitre,
Alice Duhon-Ross McCallum,
Judith Blakely, and H. Prentice Baptiste

ROWMAN & LITTLEFIELD
Lanham • Boulder • New York • London

Published by Rowman & Littlefield
An imprint of The Rowman & Littlefield Publishing Group, Inc.

4501 Forbes Boulevard, Suite 200, Lanham, Maryland 20706
www.rowman.com

86-90 Paul Street, London EC2A 4NE, United Kingdom

Copyright © 2023 by Ashraf Esmail, Abul Pitre, Alice Duhon-Ross, Judith Blakely, and H. Prentice Baptiste

All rights reserved. No part of this book may be reproduced in any form or by any electronic or mechanical means, including information storage and retrieval systems, without written permission from the publisher, except by a reviewer who may quote passages in a review.

British Library Cataloguing in Publication Information Available

Library of Congress Cataloging-in-Publication Data

Names: Esmail, Ashraf, editor. | Pitre, Abul, editor. | Duhon-Ross McCallum, Alice, editor. | Blakely, Judith, editor. | Baptiste, H. Prentice, editor.
Title: Literacy, vocabulary, and acculturation : a critical education triangle for English language learners / edited by Ashraf Esmail, Abul Pitre, Alice Duhon-Ross McCallum, Judith Blakely, and H. Prentice Baptiste.
Description: Lanham : Rowman & Littlefield, [2023] | Series: National Association for Multicultural Education (NAME) series | Summary: "This book provides strong, diverse context that supports educators in driving theory to practice when engaging with English Language Learners"—Provided by publisher.
Identifiers: LCCN 2023000976 (print) | LCCN 2023000977 (ebook) | ISBN 9781475872613 (cloth) | ISBN 9781475872620 (paperback) | ISBN 9781475872637 (epub)
Subjects: LCSH: English language—Study and teaching—Foreign speakers. | English language—Study and teaching—Social aspects. | Critical pedagogy. | LCGFT: Essays.
Classification: LCC PE1128.A2 L5333 2023 (print) | LCC PE1128.A2 (ebook) | DDC 428.0071—dc23/eng/20230316
LC record available at https://lccn.loc.gov/2023000976
LC ebook record available at https://lccn.loc.gov/2023000977

To all teachers who work with English Language Learners. May you find the ultimate reward that working with these students can bring.

Contents

Acknowledgments — ix

Introduction: Using Your Authentic Voice Through Language — xi
  Camacia Smith-Ross, EdD

Chapter 1: Beyond the Strategies: Supporting English Language Learners — 1
  David Parker

Chapter 2: Negotiating Possibilities for Teaching English Learners: A Critical Conversation Between Language Separation and Translanguaging — 11
  Kevin Donley

Chapter 3: Improving Mathematics Outcomes for English Language Learners Through Implementation of the Elementary Mathematics Initiative — 19
  Cliff Chestnutt and Andrea Smith

Chapter 4: Evolving the Language We Use: Interrupting Deficit Narratives About Multilingual Learners and Emergent Bilingual Students — 27
  Leah M. Mortenson

Chapter 5: English Language Bilingualism — 39
  Judith A. Orth and Kathleen M. Hargiss

Chapter 6: Positioning English Language Learners for Mathematical Success — 47
  Erin Smith

Chapter 7: Educational Journeys: Youth Voices as the Impetus for Social Justice Curriculum in Latinx Multilingual Classrooms — 53
  Rubén A. González

Chapter 8: Linking Multicultural Education With Best Practices for
   Multilingual Students 63
Renee Shank and Lin Wu

Chapter 9: Beyond Language: A Sociocultural Approach to K–12
   English Language Teaching and Learning 73
Immaculée Harushimana

Chapter 10: Becoming "Talent Scouts": Identifying Gifted Potential
   in English Learners 85
Holly D. Glaser and Erica C. Meadows

Chapter 11: Introducing Translanguaging as Pedagogy: Unpacking
   Preservice ESL Teachers' Language Ideologies and Practices 93
Nuo Xu and Verónica E. Valdez

Chapter 12: Characteristics of English Language Learners 101
Nan Li and Courtney A. Howard

Chapter 13: A Need for Taiwanese Indigenous Immigrant Literature 109
Hsiao-Ching Lin and Antonette Aragon

Chapter 14: Lessons and Transformations From the
   Borderlands: Preparing Educators to Support Emerging
   Bilinguals 117
Michele L. McConnell and Kelly Metz-Matthews

Chapter 15: Strategies for Moving From Learning English,
   Bilingual Education to a More Inclusive Multilingual Education 127
Georgina Y. García and Jan Perry Evenstad

Chapter 16: Real Teachers Teaching Real Students: Where Theory
   Meets Practice—Learning English in Secondary Schools 139
Glori Hodge Smith

Chapter 17: Creating Social Change for English Language Learners
   by Improving Access to Grade-Level Instruction 149
*Charity Funfe Tatah Mentan, Darrell Peterson, Yi-Chen Wu,
Kristin Kline Liu, and Kym O'Donnell*

Chapter 18: Binds and Unravels: Science Teachers Deepening
   Learning for English Language Learners 157
Analis Carattini-Ruiz

About the Editors and Contributors 169

Acknowledgments

In 2012, a unique chapter in the history of NAME was forged when the series editors and Dr. Rose Duhon-Sells met with the Rowman & Littlefield team to finalize arrangements for the series. Under the visionary leadership of Dr. Rose Duhon-Sells, the NAME series became a reality, paving the way for transformative scholarship that could improve the quality of education in the United States and abroad for diverse student populations. The editors for this book are appreciative of the Rowman & Littlefield Education (RLE) Team: Tom Koerner, Carlie Wall, and Kira Hall. A special thanks to Nancy Evans, a former member of the RLE team, who organized the initial meetings for the NAME series and to Sara Jubar for making the series a reality. The editors would like to thank all of the contributors to this volume for their interest and hard work on this important topic, English Language Learners.

Introduction

Using Your Authentic Voice Through Language

Camacia Smith-Ross, EdD

> There is power in allowing yourself to be known and heard, in owning your unique story, in using your authentic voice.
>
> —Michelle Obama

Language is a crucial building block of one's culture. According to Stanford University, in 2019, there were over 7,000 known languages worldwide. Language as we know it, is the primary method of communication and expression which allows us to interact with others and develop relationships in effective linguistic communities whereby we live, work, play, and thrive.

One of the most difficult circumstances of language is not being able to effectively communicate due to a barrier. Not only do these barriers exist but are being increasingly common in living and learning environments. Language barriers can provoke frustration, conflict, and emotional stress when there is no real solution to address the need. It continues to become our responsibility to ensure such barriers don't create biases which may perpetuate unintentional stereotypes.

As we seek apparent solutions, it is worth mentioning that intense research correlates a large number of language barriers associated with school-aged immigrant children and their families who struggled to escape harsh living conditions and poverty by seeking asylum and/or citizenship in the United States. Schools are operating to provide much needed academic support for reducing language barriers and providing foundational skills in literacy and numeracy for English Language Learners (ELL) to circumvent upsurges in poverty charged statistics.

Having command of the second language increases the student's ability to function and interact with others without embarrassment, improves motivation, and decreases the amount of emotional stress that can persist. Culturally, we must macroscopically recognize the ELL student has become the "new kid" in many school systems in the United States, out-pacing the native English speaker in many schools.

As an amenable solution, language immersion programs were concurrently developed for students to gain rapid fluency in the second language and for economic and social prosperity. Core subject teaching was taught in the second language instead of teaching the language in isolation. Students were encouraged to utilize the second language when communicating to reinforce learned subject matter.

While immersion programs have shown some success, they have become archaic with much needed reformation to truly capture the essence of assisting the ELL student with attainment of being a fully proficient bilingual. Now an added layer hovers, the Covid-19 Pandemic, which brings about a learning shift that keeps demanding educational professionals reassess teaching strategies that support student learning and assessment to full bilingualism.

As we recognize the challenges associated with students using their authentic voice, ongoing assistance has to be provided to support the ELL student. Staffing, curriculum, and program articulation obstacles must be addressed with minimum resistance. Learner-centered activities with real-world tasks can only enhance a developmentally appropriate curriculum. ELL students must feel secure in their new learning environments before student-centered learning can take place. Remember, there is no one-size-fits-all approach to educating ELL students. The challenge remains, and we must unlock doors of opportunity, promise, and hope by shaping their quality educational experiences early on.

In retrospect, there is a sociocultural and economic gain linked with increasing the proficiency of ELL students that can no longer be minimized or placed on hold. Increasing the ELL global footprint will allow societies and cultures to truly begin to value bilingualism. Experiences will become enriched and our worldview will become expansive.

Chapter 1

Beyond the Strategies

Supporting English Language Learners

David Parker

Exploring teachers' perceptions, attitudes, and explicit beliefs toward inclusion and teaching of English Language Learners has primarily focused on observable behaviors such as self-reporting, observation, case studies, and sometimes, student statements (Harrison & Lakin, 2018). However, there is an area of beliefs that can have a greater impact on the perception, attitude, and behaviors of teachers of English Language Learners (ELL). Implicit bias can influence teachers' perceptions and can directly impact instruction in a negative manner. For a teacher of English Language Learners to be the best they can be, examining implicit bias and its impact on teaching is essential.

Conversations with novice teachers focusing on their chosen profession indicate they are often filled with great intentions to make a positive difference in the lives of their students. Too often the best of intentions are altered by tangible and restrictive limitations of the realities within the profession. Issues of salary, leadership support, and classroom size can have a negative impact on the profession, all of which are outside of teachers' control.

Then there are intangible obstacles such as implicit bias that may influence intentions and result in lowered academic success for students. Implicit bias is the obstacle that disrupts learning and yet is seldom discussed within teacher education or professional development (Harper, 2019).

Too often professional development and discussions about implicit bias have been found to be painful, stressful, and, some would say, unhelpful (Chamorro-Premuzic, 2020). That does not need to be the case. This chapter will examine implicit bias from the perspective of bias as something that we all have, discuss how bias can impact teaching English Language Learners, and explore ways to reduce the bias effect.

IMPLICIT BIAS

Implicit bias refers to the automatic associations that people may make about individuals or groups (Banaji & Greenwald, 2013). These associations may influence behaviors as well as the creation and carrying out of policies. As a result of the influenced behavior or policies, people or institutions may be perceived to be explicitly prejudiced, even when their intentions are not.

The traditional belief was that behaviors that individuals and institutions demonstrated that had a discriminatory effect on others were conscious patterns.

To be clear, in actuality, everyone has bias, with no exception. Having bias is not a character flaw. Bias is a way the brain deals with all of the information that comes into it each moment. The problem comes in with how each of us chooses to allow bias to affect our behaviors, perceptions, and policy creation.

Implicit bias has far-reaching generational implications on behaviors, perceptions, and expectations. It may result in demoralizing behaviors becoming a part of the culture of an institution or community and being accepted as the way things are done. These behaviors can lead to lowered self-perception and efficacy of the individual or group who are victims of the discrimination from the behaviors. Finally, implicit bias may impact the level of expectation of the individual or group of themselves and by the greater community.

The Impact of Implicit Bias

Implicit bias has an impact on each individual within and associated with the educational community. Agarwal-Ragnath (cited in Ferlazzo, 2017) indicated classrooms are fully impacted by implicit bias. Classroom walls, teacher body language, resources available, teacher expectations, and relationships created with students and their families all can be influenced by implicit bias and give a clear message as to how you may feel about them.

Implicit bias impacts the entire educational culture, which can result in inequities for some and advantages for others. "Bias is woven through culture like a silver cord woven through cloth. In some lights, it's brightly visible. In others, it's hard to distinguish. And your position relative to that glinting thread determines whether you see it at all" (Carter, 2017; as cited in Nordell, 2017).

Regarding English Language Learners, implicit bias is manifested in unique patterns of assumptions and behaviors that influence perception, teaching, and policy. Berg (2013) described an overall reduced impression of the intellectual abilities of students in English-language learning programs compared to students for whom English is spoken at home. In addition,

Berg (2013) indicated that there is a perception that ELL students cannot learn academic content presented in English until they have mastered the English language.

Umansky and Dumont (2019) conducted research over several years with two thousand students from grades K–12 and an equal number of teachers. This study focused on teacher perception of students' academic skills. The research showed that a majority of the teachers had higher perception of students' academic skills when the student came from a home where English was the main language spoken.

DEFICIT THINKING

The United States is becoming increasingly more diverse. The overall demographics of the United States are changing as cities, small towns, rural areas, and suburbs are becoming more diverse (Pugach, 2009). With this increasing diversity comes a wider range of languages spoken as the central language at home and at school. One example of this diversity can be found in one school district where over 150 different languages are spoken. This school district is not in a large urban area but is in a medium-size southwestern state (Lingualinx, n.d.).

In cases where teachers and the culture of the school view English Language Learners as having no, or limited value, erroneous assumptions are made regarding what the ELL student has to contribute. This thinking creates what is known as a deficit model perception of the student. This deficit model impacts the overall belief system, delivery of instruction, and culture of the educational community (Pugach, 2009).

Educational policies can impact students in a negative or positive way depending on context and interpretation of the policy. Deficit-thinking policies that focus on vocabulary or language may be embedded at the macro-level of the policy (Palmer & Witanapatirana, 2020).

Teacher perception of diversity has a profound impact on instruction. In the case of language, Umansky and Dumont (2019) indicated that being classified as an English Language Learner has a long-lasting negative impact on student achievement and future success. This outcome can be traced to three specific areas of ELL students: (1) students are linguistically isolated, (2) students are placed in lower-performance-level classes, and (3) students are placed with a greater number of inexperienced teachers (Umansky & Dumont, 2019). Experienced teachers who incorporate their students' lived experiences into their instruction create a motivated and inclusive learning environment (Pugach, 2009).

Some questions to consider:

- How do you incorporate the ELL lived experiences into your delivery of instruction?
- How do you go about learning about your students' experiences?
- What are the opportunities to share this diverse teaching perspective with your colleagues?

CREATING A NEW EDUCATIONAL COMMUNITY CULTURE

Ideally, the journey of creating a culture in an educational community should incorporate the entire school. Issues of inclusion, acceptance, and belonging should be woven into every aspect of the school. This journey should not be the exclusive responsibility of teachers of English Language Learners. There may be times when the journey becomes filled with obstacles, detours, and occasional shortcuts.

Occasionally, some have attempted shortcuts on the journey by way of creating campaigns with slogans, posters, shirts, or sampling foods of different cultures, all of which have a brief start and end date. These occasional "celebrating differences" activities may lead to the erroneous belief that these celebrations adequately fulfill responsibilities to support students' diversity (Pugach, 2009). These actions that scratch the surface often lead the community in a different direction from the intended goal, resulting in a feeling of being lost.

NORTH STAR

One night when a seasoned family camper was leading an overnight camping trip in the Catskill Mountains of northern New York, he was asked a very important question by an eager group of young cousins sitting around their campfire. They had asked about how not to get lost in the woods at night. He responded that they should find the North Star. Once it is located, always be aware of its location. He continued to explain if they know where the North Star is, it can always help to keep them on track, and they would never lose their way.

Finding your school's North Star can be a way to orient your school's culture and climate to become more inclusive and welcoming. Following are some suggestions that can be like a North Star on your school's journey.

REVISIT MISSION STATEMENT

Creating and sustaining an educational community that is supportive, accepting, and inclusive requires a goal that expresses where the community is headed. Each of the many members of the community will have a role in achieving the goal. Clarity of focus, intentional design, and consistency are key influences to helping the educational community to remain on course of its expressed goals.

Mission statements are a guide. They are a representation of the beliefs and values of an educational community. They are the "why we do what we do" statements. Examine your mission statement and ask yourself these questions:

- What am I and each person in this organization responsible for in making our mission visible?
- Do I know my role and do my colleagues know their roles in carrying out our mission?

In professional conversations with employees, it is amazing the number of times they have expressed that they have no idea of the mission of their place of employment.

Here are additional questions that can be asked as your organization revisits its mission statement.

- How does the mission statement of my school relate to inclusion and acceptance?
- What behaviors are directly related to and impact the mission statement?
- What is my responsibility in making this statement reality?

When there is a lack of alignment between the stated mission and the behaviors of employees and administration, this can result in a work environment with reduced trust, more confusion, and limited energy and effort.

REVIEW EXISTING POLICIES

Policies are like a navigation system. At their core, they are the way expectations are communicated as to how each person within the educational community should treat each other and stakeholders. The policies need to be intentional in their design. Some policies may have been in place for years. There may be a need to recalculate the contents of a policy in order to reflect changes in the current workforce and cultural expectations.

Here are some questions to ask:

- When were policies relating to inclusion created and reviewed? Who created and reviewed them?
- Are there policies related to educator behavior toward all members of the school?
- How are these policies monitored?
- How is the effectiveness of the policy assessed?

ENGAGE IN ONGOING PROFESSIONAL DEVELOPMENT

Professional development needs to be current and relevant to the needs of the educational community. The professional development needs to be intentional, meaningful, and compassionate. This ongoing development should go beyond training in that it should include developing new insights to incorporate into the educators' individual teaching styles. This learning should also include support to educators as they experience challenges as their knowledge increases.

Here are some questions to ask:

- Is the professional development designed for my educational community?
- What is the ongoing support offered as part of the professional development?
- What is the growth potential for your school community with this new knowledge?

ASSESS CONTINUOUS IMPROVEMENT CYCLES

Consistent examination of the path selected is crucial to staying on course toward creating and sustaining the chosen goals. Assessing goals should occur throughout the year(s) and should be examined from a variety of perspectives, including students, families, educators, administrators, and community members. Each of these groups may have a different perception of the same environment.

Here are some questions to ask:

- How will new learning be assessed?
- Which stakeholders are involved in the assessment process?
- How can new knowledge be demonstrated?

INTENT AND IMPACT

Occasionally there may be situations when something said is not heard in the way that it was intended or a behavior is perceived as something different than was intended. In other words, the intent and impact are not the same. George Bernard Shaw (n.d.) said, "The single biggest problem in communication is the illusion that it has taken place." What is communicated is not always aligned with our conscious thoughts. The following are three examples observed at schools when intent and impact were not aligned.

- Students are called on with greater frequency based on gender. The intent could be that a teacher may call on boys more because the teacher knows that the girls know the answers. The impact is that the girls feel ignored.
- Classroom support is given to some students more often than others. The intent is to support those students who need extra support. The impact is that other students who need support as well go without that support.
- A comment in class seems to upset a few students while the others seem unaffected by the comment. The intent may be a comment that is said in a joking manner. The impact is that the joking comment is offensive to some of the students.

Sometimes intent and impact may be different due to implicit bias. When there is a conflict between intent and impact, someone may be harmed. The behavior of the person who engaged in the activity or statement may come into question. This can cause the person whose actions are being questioned to become defensive. The reason for the defensiveness may be because the impact may not be aligned with how the person in question sees themselves or wants others to think of them.

Hodges and Myers (2007) stated that the ability to see from the others' perspectives is an act of cognitive empathy, which they describe as the ability to perceive and understand the emotions of another person. In a situation when there is a clear disconnect between intent and impact, using cognitive empathy can be a tool toward healing an experience.

It is possible to develop and strengthen your cognitive empathy skills. Borges (2016) stated that developing this ability is one that can be learned. The first step to cognitive empathy is self-awareness. Before you connect with somebody else, it's incredibly important to have a strong awareness of yourself and your own emotions. Being self-aware can help determine which emotions are your own and which emotions are those of other people.

The second step is developing an emotional connection to the situation and the feelings expressed. An emotional connection allows you to have the perspective of feeling the situation.

The third step is to take an action step. Here, the teacher, along with a trusted colleague, can explore their intent and its impact in their teaching to increase their alignment between intent and impact. Each of these steps can lead to improving the relationships among teachers, students, and families as well as healing or preventing a painful situation.

Our places of learning are shifting to become more dynamic and diverse educational communities. With that shift, there is a need to intentionally create and sustain environments that are inclusive as well as authentically focused on the success of English Language Learners and, indeed, all learners. There are barriers that exist that create obstacles to successful student belonging and achievement.

The intent of this chapter was to invite educators to explore implicit bias, perhaps one of the biggest barriers to acceptance and student achievement. Implicit bias can and does influence perception, beliefs, behavior, and the creation of policy.

It is hoped that the impact of this chapter will lead to an increased development in individual and organizational self-awareness related to beliefs and behaviors. The use of researched-based practices to assess how relationships with students are created and maintained is encouraged. These practices can lead to creating inclusive and welcoming spaces for all learners.

REFERENCES

Banaji, M. R., & Greenwald, A. G. (2013). *Blindspot: Hidden biases of good people*. Delacorte Press.

Berg, N. (2013). Busting ELL myths: Safety helps overcome stereotypes in this ESOL class. *Teaching Tolerance*. https://www.tolerance.org/magazine/busting-ell-myths

Borges, E. (2016). *The secret weapon in deconstructing unconscious bias in the workplace*. https://www.smartbrief.com/original/2016/09/secret-weapon-deconstructing-unconscious-bias-workplace

Chamorro-Premuzic, T. (2020, January 13). Why implicit bias training doesn't work at companies. *Japan Times*. https://www.japantimes.co.jp/opinion/2020/01/13/commentary/world-commentary/implicit-bias-training-doesnt-work-companies

Ferlazzo, L. (2017, September 23). *How can teachers approach race and bias in the classroom?* https://www.edweek.org/teaching-learning/opinion-response-approach-race-implicit-bias-by-listening-to-students/2017/09

Harper, A. (2019). *Should districts require implicit bias training for educators?* https://www.educationdive.com/news/should-districts-require-implicit-bias-training-for-educators/555524

Harrison, J., & Lakin, J. (2018). Mainstream teachers' implicit beliefs about English Language Learners: An implicit association test study of teacher beliefs. *Journal of Language, Identity & Education, 17*(2), 85–102, https://doi.org/10.1080/15348458.2017.1397520

Hodges, S. D., & Myers, M. W. (2007). Empathy. *Encyclopedia of Social Psychology,* 291–293. http://web.a.ebscohost.com.ezproxy.lib.utah.edu/ehost/ebookviewer/ebook?sid=1f3f40ad-6141-4411-a95d-4b8e7efe2287%40sessionmgr4008&vid=0&format=EB

Lingualinx. (n.d.). Retrieved January 5, 2022, from https://www.lingualinx.com/case-studies/salt-lake-city-public-schools

Nordell, J. (2017, May). Is this how discrimination ends? *The Atlantic.* https://www.theatlantic.com/science/archive/2017/05/unconscious-bias-training/525405

Palmer, D., & Witanapatirana, K. (2020). Exposing bias through a deficit thinking lens using content-analysis of macro level policies. *Research in Educational Policy and Management, 2*(1), 23–39. https://doi.org/10.46303/repam.01.02.2

Pugach, M. C. (2009). *Because teaching matters: An introduction to the profession.* John Wiley & Sons.

Shaw, G. B. (n.d.). *George Bernard Shaw quotes.* Retrieved January 5, 2022, from https://www.brainyquote.com/authors/george-bernard-shaw-quotes

Umansky, I., & Dumont, H. (2019, December 3). Do teachers have biased academic perceptions of their English learner students? *Brookings.* https://www.brookings.edu/blog/brown-center-chalkboard/2019/12/03/do-teachers-have-biased-academic-perceptions-of-their-english-learner-students

Chapter 2

Negotiating Possibilities for Teaching English Learners

A Critical Conversation Between Language Separation and Translanguaging

Kevin Donley

Every public school classroom in the United States is shaped by a political and ideological tension between the historical currents of immigration and current trends toward globalization. Caught in between are the millions of students coming from homes where English is not the dominant language used—commonly referred to as English Learners (EL) (Ramírez et al., 2018). Teachers across the country are challenged with navigating linguistic diversity, regardless of instructional context, and therefore must think of themselves as multilingual teachers to effectively support the multilingual and multicultural development of ELs (Fu et al., 2019).

There is a growing need for critically, linguistically, and culturally conscious teachers who embrace their roles as agents of social change to empower their EL students (Palmer et al., 2019). However, the diversity of classroom contexts in which EL students learn means that there cannot be a standardized, one-size-fits-all approach. The ability of teachers to act for social change is supported by access to information and tools to interrogate their own classroom contexts. Learning about harmful monolingual ideologies or inclusive multilingual pedagogies is indeed important, but teachers must apply this knowledge within an almost entirely monolingual schooling system (Deroo & Ponzio, 2019).

For example, translanguaging is a framework that centers the dynamic, flexible, and creative ways that ELs draw on the entirety of their multilingual resources to both learn and interact (García et al., 2017). While this stance can be potentially transformative for ELs and their access to learning (Kleyn & García, 2018), it does not fit easily into the dominant framework that treats language-mixing as a barrier to academic achievement for EL students, commonly referred to as language separation (Palmer et al., 2014). A critical awareness of competing pedagogical approaches for ELs can be a starting point for creating effective learning environments and relevant assessment practices that better fit our goals for social change and EL empowerment.

This chapter demonstrates how these competing frameworks can be put in critical conversation with each other for the purpose of reimagining equitable multilingual strategies for teaching EL students. Framed by a research process developed from an undergraduate multilingual education course, it explores how a group of 20 future teachers put these two competing frameworks in critical conversation to creatively negotiate the possibilities for translanguaging pedagogy in the context of language separation classrooms. Therefore, this chapter will present this process for teachers of ELs to do the same according to the language frameworks that shape their classroom contexts, by following these three steps:

- Step 1: Define language frameworks based on five central questions:
  - How is *language* defined?
  - How is *language competency* defined?
  - How is it assessed?
  - What is the role of the teacher?
  - What is the role of the student?
- Step 2: Put each framework in critical conversation to identify incompatibilities, synergies, and areas of negotiation, in relation to the central questions
- Step 3: Negotiate and reimagine the possibilities for EL-centered instructional strategies in language separation contexts

STEP 1: DEFINING LANGUAGE FRAMEWORKS

Many teachers are already asking important questions about the benefits of inclusive and culturally responsive pedagogies for ELs and their access to education (Polat et al., 2019). To answer these questions, teachers must also interrogate how multilingualism works, for what purposes, and the difference between teaching languages and teaching about languages (de Jong et al., 2013). Therefore, the first step toward creating equitable and effective instructional strategies and assessment practices for ELs is to critically interrogate any language framework based on how language, competency, and the roles of teachers and students are defined.

In the research that informs this chapter, the group of future teachers began by collaboratively defining the framework of language separation based on five central questions. This is a summary of the product of multiple group-work sessions of writing, providing feedback, and revising the answers to each question. The citations for this chapter provide a helpful reading list for a deeper exploration of both frameworks.

1. *How is* language *defined?* Language is considered a fixed object that can be acquired. It is given stability and structure by the rules of grammar and syntax. Languages are tools for meaning making and learning. Different languages can be boxed into clearly defined categories. Bilingualism is treated as double or parallel monolingualism.
2. *How is* language competency *defined?* Language competency is considered a skill or ability centered on academic proficiency and fluency. There is a strong focus on literacy and comprehension. While cross-linguistic transfer is possible, bilingual competency is best achieved by developing each language separately.
3. *How is language competency evaluated?* Language competency is assessed in the standardized terms of academic literacy and communicative proficiency. Adherence to the rules of proper grammar and syntax is prioritized. Multilingual competency is mostly evaluated monolingually, meaning the measurable literacy and proficiency criteria for each language are assessed separately.
4. *What is the role of the student?* The role of the student is to acquire and possess the skills associated with linguistic proficiency and academic literacy. Their learning and participation should conform to the standardized criteria of appropriate language practices. Multilingual students are to acquire different languages separately and linearly, striving for cultural awareness through academic multilingualism.
5. *What is the role of the teacher?* The teacher's role is to develop the language and literacy skills of their students by acting as models of knowledge and conveyers of content. One of their responsibilities is to police the academic standards of language use in the classroom. Multilingual teachers should essentially act as monolingual models, which often means disciplining informal language-mixing practices.

The group then followed the same collaborative process of writing, feedback, and revision for defining *translanguaging*.

1. *How is* language *defined?* Languages are not viewed as objects or tools to be acquired. Academic languages are political constructions that cannot be boxed into clearly defined categories and do not reflect real-life language practices. Focus should instead be on "languaging" as a process and practice. Multilingualism is a dynamic, fluid, flexible process in which students draw on a unified linguistic repertoire.
2. *How is* language competency *defined?* Language competency is the strategic and multimodal negotiation of the entirety of one's linguistic repertoire. Academic literacy is just one of many relevant multimodal practices. More important is social interaction that is culturally and critically aware. Multilingual competency is naturally dynamic, fluid, and flexible.
3. *How is language competency evaluated?* Language competency is evaluated multimodally in terms of cultural fluency, metalinguistic awareness, and as a practical, flexible, and creative practice. This is done through multi-staged activities and projects. Monolingual assessments of multilingual competency fail to fully capture the multiplicity of experiences, knowledges, and literacies that students bring.
4. *What is the role of the student?* Students should be considered co-learners and equal participants in the creation of inclusive learning spaces. Their role is to engage flexibly with the content and curriculum, taking creative risks to demonstrate knowledge flexibly. Multilingual students should do so collaboratively while drawing on the collective linguistic repertoire of the classroom.
5. *What is the role of the teacher?* Teachers are not the only knowledge models in the classroom. They are co-learners and equal participants in creating inclusive spaces and engage critically with power dynamics related to language and culture. They are pedagogically flexible and remain open to unplanned curriculum practices. Multilingual teachers encourage, support, and model flexible and creative languaging.

STEP 2: PUTTING LANGUAGE FRAMEWORKS IN CRITICAL CONVERSATION

With the understanding that a language separation framework shapes most public-school classrooms, the next step in the process is to explore the incompatibilities, synergies, and areas of negotiation between it and translanguaging, in relation to each of the five central questions. Following a similar collaborative process of group-work, this critical conversation between competing frameworks served as the basis for the negotiation of translanguaging strategies within the context of language separation classrooms. What follows is a summary of their conclusions.

At the most basic level, language separation and translanguaging are founded on mutually exclusive definitions of *language*, as the former defines *language* as a structural, categorizable object, while the latter redefines *language* as a fluid, uncategorizable practice. The former narrowly considers language competency in standardized, academic terms, while the latter moves the focus of competency and assessment to the strategic, flexible negotiation of all linguistic resources.

Finally, the former positions teachers as authoritative language models and students as conformers to academic standards, while the latter transforms the teacher-student relationship to position both as equal co-learners and creative risk takers. Despite these incompatibilities, there are various synergies and areas of negotiation that are worth highlighting.

Foundationally, both frameworks view language as a tool, resource, and right for EL students and acknowledge the relationship between language, culture, and identity formation. Interaction and communication are valued practices of language within each. There is a value in language separation for practice-based language pedagogies, though not as strongly as in translanguaging. While a focus on the grammatical rules of language may be too narrow in language separation, it should not be entirely ignored from a translanguaging perspective. An important question becomes: *How can EL pedagogies move away from a focus on individual languages and language users toward collaborative or collective languaging?*

Regarding language competency, both frameworks understand language as a multimodal ability or skill and place value on metalinguistic awareness. They each value cultural awareness in relation to language and language learning. While language separation focuses narrowly on literacy as competency, it is not entirely disregarded by translanguaging. Rather, literacy is recognized as just one of many relevant communicative skills. An important question becomes: *to what extent should literacy skills define the benchmarks for language competency?*

This provokes valuable similarities and areas of negotiation about how language competency should be assessed. Both frameworks integrate criteria related to multimodality, oral language skills, successful meaning-making, and metalinguistic awareness, valuing them as important indicators of language competency. They disagree, however, on the role of standardized, monolingual assessment focused only on academic literacy. While translanguaging decenters concepts like target language zones or measurable grammar skills, they are still relevant, although not primary assessment concepts. An important question becomes: *How can flexible languaging be assessed, and what does its equitable assessment look like?*

Finally, both frameworks position teachers as facilitators of learning in the classroom and as important role-players in the language development of EL students. The responsibility of teachers includes advocacy and support for inclusive learning spaces that embrace multiple languages in classroom practice and integrate them into instruction. The role of students, in each framework, is to act as a language broker while collaboratively engaging with the content and curriculum. The significant area of negotiation here is the extent to which teachers and students are positioned as co-learners. For example, teachers must still model language and culture practices, evaluate student learning, and navigate unplanned and flexible curriculum. Also, students are still expected to demonstrate knowledge and become more culturally aware. An important question, then, is: *In what practical ways can students be given more power to negotiate classroom content and curriculum?*

Within classroom contexts of language separation, the most difficult challenge is to embrace fluidity and flexibility in terms of language practices, competency assessment, and pedagogy. A strong focus on strategic languaging and creative risk-taking, in both practice and assessment, is also difficult to fit within a language separation curriculum.

While ideally there is space within a language separation framework to move students toward the position of equal co-learners with teachers, what this looks like in practice may be difficult to imagine and thus deserves further attention. While this kind of critical conversation between frameworks may generate more questions than answers, it serves as a valuable basis for reimagining translanguaging strategies for teaching ELs, which is the focus of the next section.

STEP 3: NEGOTIATING AND REIMAGINING TRANSLANGUAGING INSTRUCTION FOR EL STUDENTS

After defining each framework and negotiating them through critical conversation, the final step is to reimagine ways to put this knowledge into action. This section reflects on how the future teachers worked within and beyond the boundaries of language separation and translanguaging toward creative and potentially more equitable instructional strategies for EL students. They began with two group brainstorming sessions, and areas of negotiation were used as starting points for discussion, and after each session, they reflected on both the successes and challenges of reimagining translanguaging strategies.

They felt successful in negotiating literacy as just one of many communicative skills, integrating multimodality and creating inclusive spaces. They also recognized that language separation practices can still play a role in the classroom but felt the need to decenter these practices to pass more co-learning power to EL students. On the other hand, they reported difficulties in redefining language competency, aligning translanguaging with state standards and criteria, and avoiding monolingual assessment practices. While they felt that narrowing a broad concept like translanguaging to concrete instructional and assessment practices is very difficult, the future teachers generated creative and flexible reimaginations of translanguaging strategies for teaching EL students in monolingual or language separation classroom contexts.

For example, one group integrated multimodality and student co-learning through an activity oriented around creating and sharing graphic novels, posing questions about flexible and multimodal assessment practices, and disrupting the idea that language is structured and purely lexical. Another group aimed to disrupt teachers as monolingual models and the only authority by integrating a student-led daily peer-learning, mutual-support, or small-group study time, in which students are grouped to the best extent possible in ways that multiple languages can be mutually supported. Teachers offering guiding questions primarily allow for fluidity in these co-learning sessions.

This provoked questions about how EL students could co-generate their expectations and responsibilities for this classroom time. For example, a group aimed to balance academic literacy and translanguaging flexibility by generating an activity that asked EL students to create bilingual picture books, and for them to determine the linguistic boundaries of their books. In this activity, students could begin with wordless picture books, engage with the story orally and flexibly, then write a bilingual version of the story while integrating both multiple languages cohesively. These examples make clear, though, that reimagining concrete assessment practices remains a problem.

While challenging monolingualism in curriculum development is unquestionably difficult (Barros et al., 2020), the examples generated by the future teachers in this research highlight the potential value of this process of framework definition, critical negotiation, and creative reimagination for any language-based pedagogical approaches that teachers of ELs may call on or encounter. The first step is vital for critically and consciously interrogating any language framework. The second step is necessary for finding spaces of flexibility in which to integrate flexible, equity-oriented instructional practices for ELs, serving as the basis for teachers of ELs to enact their agency in redefining and reimagining their instructional practices in ways that empower the agency of EL students to do the same.

What has been presented in this chapter thus serves as a tool for current and future teachers of ELs, especially in monolingual instructional contexts, to create instruction and assessment practices that support social change and EL empowerment. Through this process, teachers engage in a reflexive practice of defining, juxtaposing, and negotiating how to fit language-conscious pedagogy to the flexible realities and needs of their EL students.

Keeping in mind that language is the primary identifier of an EL student, teachers must be critically conscious of how dominant pedagogical approaches can be rooted in potentially harmful monolingual assumptions that narrow the instructional focus on ELs to literacy and academic achievement. Critical interrogation, starting with how language, competency, and student and teacher roles are generally defined, can be generative of practical ways to promote the agency of EL students through flexible and multilingual pedagogies, such as translanguaging.

REFERENCES

Barros, S., Domke, L. M., Symons, C., & Ponzio, C. (2020). Challenging monolingual ways of looking at multilingualism: Insights for curriculum development in teacher preparation. *Journal of Language, Identity & Education, 20*(4), 239–254. doi:10.1080/15348458.2020.1753196

de Jong, E. J., Harper, C. A., & Coady, M. R. (2013). Preparing mainstream teachers for CLD students: Enhancing the knowledge and skills that teachers of CLDs must have. *Theory Into Practice, 52*(2), 89–97.

Deroo, M. R., & Ponzio, C. (2019). Confronting ideologies: A discourse analysis of in-service teachers' translanguaging stance through an ecological lens. *Bilingual Research Journal, 42*(2), 214–231.

Fu, D., Hadjioannou, X., & Zhou, X. (2019). *Translanguaging for emergent bilinguals: Inclusive teaching in the linguistically diverse classroom*. Teachers College Press.

García, O., Johnson, S., & Seltzer, K. (2017). *The translanguaging classroom. Leveraging student bilingualism for learning*. Caslon.

Kleyn, T., & García, O. (2019). Translanguaging as an act of transformation. In L. C. de Oliveira (Ed.), *The handbook of TESOL in K–12* (pp. 69–82). John Wiley & Sons.

Palmer, D., Cervantes-Soon, C., Dorner, L., & Heiman, D. (2019). Bilingualism, biliteracy, biculturalism, and critical consciousness for all: Proposing a fourth fundamental goal for two-way dual language education. *Theory Into Practice, 58*(2), 121–133. doi.org/10/1080/00405841.2019.1569376.

Palmer, D. K., Martínez, R. A., Mateus, S. G., & Henderson, K. (2014). Reframing the debate on language separation: Toward a vision for translanguaging pedagogies in the dual language classroom. *Modern Language Journal, 98*, 757–772.

Polat, N., Mahalingappa, L., Hughes, E., & Karayigit, C. (2019). Change in preservice teacher beliefs about inclusion, responsibility, and culturally responsive pedagogy for English learners. *International Multilingual Research Journal, 13*(4), 222–238.

Ramirez, P. C., Faltis, C. J., & de Jong, E. J. (2018). *Learning from emergent bilingual Latinx learners in K–12*. Routledge.

Chapter 3

Improving Mathematics Outcomes for English Language Learners Through Implementation of the Elementary Mathematics Initiative

Cliff Chestnutt and Andrea Smith

Many schools and school systems today are faced with the challenge of a gap in academic achievement between English Language Learners (ELLs) and White students. For over 2 decades, there has been no statistically significant increase in the mathematics scores of ELL students on NAEP assessments.

On the contrary, scores among White students have continued to steadily increase (National Center for Educational Statistics [NCES], 2008). While the research on the gap in achievement between ELLs and White students is extensive and diverse, multiple studies have posited instructional practices (Beecher & Sweeney, 2008), state and local policies (Cooper, 2007), and family predictors (Jerome, Hamre, and Pianta, 2009) as possible indicators for lower academic achievement in mathematics among ELLs. Essentially, families are a critical component of children's overall learning and their involvement can directly influence children's overall math achievement (Epstein & Sheldon, 2006).

Since school demographics have shifted and resulted in an increase in the number of ELLs enrolled in public schools in the United States, many schools have begun to develop viable programs aimed at improving mathematics achievement among ELLs. One such program that has been implemented at the elementary level to improve Georgia Milestones Assessment System (GMAS) scores in mathematics is the Elementary Math Initiative (EMI). The EMI was designed to increase instructional time in math and also increase the focus on problem solving, communication of mathematical thinking, the use of a variety of instructional approaches (including differentiation and enrichment), and parent involvement in math.

The EMI first began by all classrooms having a minimum of a 75-minute block each day for math instruction. After the additional instructional time was added, teachers received training on the implementation of the Everyday Math curriculum that they would be using throughout the EMI. In addition to the implementation of the Everyday Math curriculum and increased instructional differentiation, a team of teachers began to plan family math nights to encourage parental involvement.

The family math nights were held monthly, and the parents were encouraged to participate in math games with their children and were given the opportunity to discuss questions and concerns with the teachers. In monthly faculty meetings, teachers spent 15 minutes in groups discussing the overall effectiveness of the program and any areas they felt needed improvement. The purpose of this study was to determine if the implementation of the EMI impacted the number of students passing or failing the mathematics portion of the GMAS at one elementary school.

THE ACADEMIC ACHIEVEMENT GAP AND MATHEMATICS INSTRUCTION

Despite progress being made to decrease the achievement gap between ELLs and White students during the 1960s and 1970s, the academic achievement of ELLs has steadily declined since the 1980s. Although there has been some improvement in the academic achievement in ELLs over the past 3 decades, their achievement gains in relation to their White counterparts have been insignificant (Tirado & Shneyderman, 2020).

The limited academic achievement among ELLs is representative of a complex problem that should be addressed since the population of ELLs in public schools continues to increase. As such, comprehensive solutions to address the mathematics achievement gap must be addressed by all stakeholders such as teachers, school leaders, and education policymakers.

Shim (2014) suggested that ELLs face numerous academic challenges in and out of the classroom. His research indicated that, as a group, ELLs are provided with a less rigorous curriculum. Lower expectations for these students often preclude these students from participating in more advanced classes due to the lack of initial preparation.

The U.S. Department of Education indicated that approximately one fourth of ELLs participate in advanced mathematics courses compared to one half of White students (NCES, 2008). This report indicated that only 59% of ELLs took mid-level mathematics courses, 8% completed low-level courses, and

7% completed no mathematics courses at all. This lack of preparation at the early grades becomes a bigger challenge as the students move through school.

Beecher and Sweeney (2008) found that differentiating instruction through enrichment improved academic performance, whereas Mandara et al. (2009) concluded that family and social influences had a significant impact on the achievement of ELLs. Weglinsky (2004) further supported that the student achievement gap in math can be decreased through instructional practice.

Instructional practices that reduced the student achievement gap on the NAEP mathematics test were identified using a hierarchical linear model with data from 13,000 fourth graders. The study suggests that time on task, the emphasis on measurement and estimation, and an emphasis on hands-on problem solving proved to be most beneficial in reducing the achievement gap. Additionally, the study found that by using differentiation and enrichment or remediation, teachers can significantly reduce the student achievement gap (Weglinsky, 2004).

In addition to the previous studies, Little (2009) described the ever-changing expectations about mathematics in schools and specific instructional strategies to meet the needs of Latino students. Little discussed the need for individualized, differentiated instruction, increased instructional time, and application of math to the students' lives. Differentiation is implemented in a variety of ways in the classroom.

Differentiation can be achieved through flexible grouping as well as remediation and enrichment. Also, according to her study, students must receive a minimum of 1 hour a day for mathematics instruction for academic achievement to increase. With this increased instructional time, students also must be allowed to apply the math concepts they learn in class to hands-on problems to develop an in-depth understanding (Little, 2009). Overall, results from the aforementioned studies indicated that the implementation of these instructional strategies in mathematics can improve academic achievement of ELLs.

TRANSFORMING MATH INSTRUCTION THROUGH THE ELEMENTARY MATH INITIATIVE

The Elementary Math Initiative was designed to address ELLs' achievement in mathematics. The EMI was developed using the Everyday Mathematics curriculum to involve ELLs in meaningful, engaging mathematics instruction. At all elementary grade levels (K–5), the program allows students multiple opportunities to learn mathematics concepts and practice skills through interactive, hands-on problem-solving tasks.

The factors that distinguish Everyday Math from other curriculum programs are the focus on problem solving, student communication of math concepts, and increased instructional time for lessons and practice. This curriculum also balances different types of instruction (including collaboration, enrichment, and remediation), provides multiple methods for necessary skills practice, and focuses on enhanced home and school partnerships.

Hands-On Problem Solving

A primary focus of the EMI was to engage ELLs in hands-on problem solving. As discussed by English et al. (2010), schools that incorporate hands-on problems into their math curriculum and allow students to discover math concepts for themselves will see significant improvement in student achievement. Using a hands-on approach to problem solving allowed the sessions to be more engaging and promoted deeper understanding of mathematics concepts among students and parents.

The EMI used Standards for Mathematical Practice (SMP) to discuss, and a short workshop was held to explain to parents how and why the SMPs are used in mathematics. During the workshop, the group explored how students interact with SMPs by examining student work samples and classroom activities. During the family math games, parents and students also had the opportunity to discuss the mathematical practices they were engaging in.

The fraction exploration session started with discussions about the parents' knowledge of and experience with fractions. After learning about their prior knowledge, parents began exploring fractions concepts from different elementary grade levels. Fraction explorations began by having the parents participating in a candy sort to address sets. The session then moved into other fraction comparison activities using pictorial representations. These activities helped to further develop the parents' conceptual understanding of fractions and led to further exploration of concepts of fraction addition and subtraction.

A hands-on approach was implemented to help the parents develop conceptual understanding of various math concepts and how math can be used in real-world situations. This carefully planned process allowed the parents to make connections from the math concepts discussed in class to activities they were doing with their students at home. Another important focus of the sessions was discussing with parents the way they were taught math in school.

Most parents discussed learning specific procedures and memorizing facts, and this presented a challenge for some parents. Some parents in the sessions were initially hesitant to participate in what they viewed as a different, more complicated approach, but throughout the sessions most began to see the benefits of this approach for their children.

Instructional Differentiation

Additionally, the EMI introduced instructional improvements by using the enrichment and remediation pieces of the Everyday Math curriculum. Before the implementation of the EMI, all students in the school were taught the same lessons using direct instruction. According to Weglinsky (2004), improving teaching through classroom enrichment and remediation is critical in the improvement of student achievement in math. During implementation, students participated in small-group math instruction to meet their individual academic needs.

In all of the classrooms participating in the EMI, students were provided remediation or enrichment opportunities based on their performance on weekly assessments and exit tickets after each lesson. Students who received a score less than 70% on assessments participated in instructional remediation through reteaching and extra practice, while students scoring above 70% were involved in review and enrichment sessions. A central focus of the differentiation component was to ensure that all teachers held high expectations for their ELL students to increase mathematics achievement.

Family Math Nights

The final element of the EMI was the development of family math nights to introduce the parents of ELLs to the math curriculum and also spend time teaching the parents how to help their students with math concepts at home properly. The math nights would occur monthly for parents, teachers, and students to work together to improve mathematics achievement.

During the family math nights, students and parents would begin by participating in a hands-on exploration of math concepts facilitated by a teacher. Following this activity, the students would join their parents for participation in math games to further develop the concepts. The games were set up in a series of rotations so that students and their families would have the opportunity to participate in four different activities.

Classroom teachers were present to teach and facilitate the games, as well as answer any questions that arose. For example, during the multiplication/division game night, families played Monster Multiplication, which is a game that uses predetermined factors. During this game, families could practice fact fluency while reasoning which factors would allow them to get four in a row.

Mathematically rich and fun family interactions occurred throughout the math nights. While playing the games, it was clear that both parents and students wanted to win the games, and the friendly competition encouraged more mathematical discussion and support for each other. Teachers were there to support the families and ask questions to extend their thinking. This allowed families that had difficulty to be successful and helped to reinforce the concepts for everyone involved, specifically the mathematical language that was introduced prior to participation in the game.

Everyone involved enjoyed games that they learned and played. Several students mentioned, "I can't wait until the next game night! I am so excited to do math with my mom." One parent also indicated, "I had no idea math could be so much fun. I am glad to learn how to play so I can support my child at home." To further support the families, all were provided with printouts of the games and math manipulatives to take home.

ELEMENTARY MATH INITIATIVE: THE CHALLENGES

Findings from the study indicated that the implementation of the Elementary Math Initiative had no statistically significant impact on the number of ELLs passing or failing the mathematics section of the GMAS. There may have been several reasons for these findings, including only 1 year of program implementation prior to testing, limited parent involvement in the program, and decreased expectations toward ELLs by some teachers. One effect on the findings of the current study is the limited parental involvement in the program.

Many of the studies discussed the significant benefits of increased parental involvement in the mathematics achievement of Latino students (Llagas, 2003; Lopez & Donovan, 2009). This may be because they were more capable of involving most parents by providing transportation and childcare for the participating families than the researchers in the current study. The present research might have shown more positive GMAS results if there had been the opportunity to involve a majority of the parents in the family game nights. Increasing the number of parents attending the program would help to provide a greater understanding of the math concepts, allowing them to work more effectively with their child at home.

An additional possible impact of the findings of this study is the decrease in teacher expectations for ELLs. During this study, many teachers expressed low expectations for the ELLs in their class and felt they would not succeed on the state GMAS test. Jerome and colleagues (2009), in their study, discussed the importance of teachers setting and maintaining high academic expectations of their ELLs. The current research might have shown an increase in results if a specific focus had been placed on teacher expectations for ELLs.

ELEMENTARY MATH INITIATIVE: THE BENEFITS

While this study indicated no statistically significant impact on standardized test scores, all teachers reported an increase in student classroom performance and engagement in class. Teachers indicated that students were more successful with classwork and homework assignments, and all students increased their overall grade in math. Teachers also discussed an increase in parent participation with their students related to mathematics.

Although the initial focus of the EMI was to address ELLs' performance on standardized testing, the academic benefits became evident during the math sessions. The program provided long-lasting mathematics learning benefits for students and parents that were able to participate. The school is continuing to implement this program while constantly evaluating and making necessary improvements to meet the needs of the school community.

Family involvement that increases learning at home and improves students' attitudes toward math can potentially increase children's math performance and improve parent-child interactions (Epstein & Sheldon, 2006). The EMI created the opportunity for parents to participate and engage in math with their children, thus providing them with additional tools to support their child at home and continuing to develop mathematical understanding. For the EMI to be successful, it was important for the school to view all ELL students and their families as partners that contribute a significant amount of knowledge and experience to the program.

An effective and engaging method of encouraging ELL families to improve math concepts at home was teaching parents specific ways to help their children and decreasing barriers to engaging families. This is exactly what the EMI provided for this school community. Teachers provided parents with hands-on activities and games to increase the confidence and ability to help their children. Connecting math concepts to the students' and parents' everyday lives allowed the teachers to help parents develop a deeper understanding of math activities to assist their children at home.

Families were taught math games that required real-world problems to extend their math learning. These games allowed parents to play a more significant role in helping all members of the family develop deeper mathematical understanding. Following the initial implementation of the EMI, 92% of the parents indicated they continued using the math games at home, indicating an increase in math engagement that will have long-lasting benefits for the families.

Academic achievement in mathematics for ELL students continues to be a challenge in schools across the United States. Increasing family involvement in the learning process is a crucial component in improving the mathematics achievement for these children. School-based programs like the EMI provide a potential framework for addressing the long-term mathematics achievement of ELL students and need to continually be developed and improved to provide access to mathematics content and learning for all students.

REFERENCES

Beecher, M., & Sweeney, S. M. (2008). Closing the achievement gap with curriculum enrichment and differentiation: One school's story. *Journal of Advanced Academics, 19*(3), 502–530.

Cooper, L. A. (2007). Why closing the research-practice gap is critical to closing student achievement gaps. *Theory Into Practice, 46*(4), 317–324.

English, L., Humble, S., & Barnes, V. (2010). Trailblazers. *Teaching Children Mathematics, 16*(7), 402–409.

Epstein, J. L., & Sheldon, S. B. (2006). Moving forward: Ideas for research on school, family, and community partnerships. In C. Conrad & R. C. Serlin (Eds.), *SAGE Handbook for Research in Education: Engaging Ideas and Enriching Inquiry* (pp. 117–138). SAGE.

Jerome, E., Hamre, B., & Pianta, R. (2009). Teacher-child relationships from kindergarten to sixth grade: Early childhood predictors of teacher perceived conflict and closeness. *Social Development, 18*(4), 915–945.

Little, M. (2009). Teaching mathematics: Issues and solutions. *Teaching Exceptional Children Plus, 6*(1), 1–15.

Llagas, C. (2003). Status and trends in the education of Hispanics. *National Center for Educational Statistics, 56*(7), 23–41.

Lopez, C., & Donovan, L. (2009). Involving Latino parents with mathematics through family math nights: A review of literature. *Journal of Latinos and Education, 8*(3), 219–230.

Mandara, J., Varner, F., Greene, N., & Richman, S. (2009). Intergenerational predictors of the Black-White achievement gap. *Journal of Educational Psychology, 101*(64), 867–878.

National Center for Educational Statistics. (2008). *Mathematics achievement of language-minority students during the elementary years*. U.S. Department of Education.

Shim, J. M. (2014). A Bourdieuian analysis: Teachers' beliefs about English Language Learners' academic challenges. *International Journal of Multicultural Education, 16*(1), 40–55.

Tirado, A., & Shneyderman, A. (2020). *Student achievement growth in early elementary grades and the persistence of the achievement gap* [Research brief]. Volume 1909. Research Services, Miami-Dade County Public Schools.

Weglinsky, H. (2004). Closing the racial achievement gap: The role of reforming instructional practice. *Education Policy Analysis Archives, 12*(64), 1–22.

Chapter 4

Evolving the Language We Use

Interrupting Deficit Narratives About Multilingual Learners and Emergent Bilingual Students

Leah M. Mortenson

OVERVIEW OF DEFICIT NARRATIVES ABOUT MULTILINGUAL LEARNERS

Deficit narratives about multilingual learners (MLLs) have been perpetuated in a number of ways, but perhaps most insidiously and commonly in the stories teachers tell to one another through informal conversations. Minoritized students are positioned as "less than" through discourses in the institution of public schooling, and these discourses often go unchallenged (Tatum, 2017).

Educators are the linchpins who perpetuate or interrupt deficit narratives, so when these ideas continue to circulate underneath our teaching, students may experience negative educational outcomes like minimized feelings of self-worth, decreased motivation in school, and lowered academic success (Bittle, 2013; Debasish, 2010; Kumaravadivelu, 2003; Morris, 2016). Students internalize the messages we communicate to them, explicitly or implicitly, so the stories we have absorbed and tell others matter.

Teachers' language attitudes are often racialized, and they may perceive minority groups negatively, which affects student learning (Kynard, 2013). Deficit language ideologies perpetuate inequities in education; simultaneously, White teachers, who comprise a majority of TESOL educators, may be seen as having racist, untrustworthy motives by minoritized students, leading to a cyclical relationship of unease and distrust, which impacts students' academic success (McBee Orzulak, 2015). There are a number of deficit narratives told in educational settings that must be examined in order for us to both understand the messaging that is circulating as well as address how we can change it.

"MLLS ARE PASSIVE"

One of the most longstanding deficit narratives about MLL students, and more specifically Asian students, is that they are "passive" (Kumaravadivelu, 2003). This typecast, and other more "positive" stereotypes of Asian students, such as that they are a "model minority," set expectations that are deterministic and generalizing (Cheryan & Bodenhausen, 2000).

Furthermore, the curricula, textbooks, and materials used in schools often contain both racial stereotypes and assimilation agendas (Kubota, 2002), which goes to show that neither the stories told about students nor the materials used to teach them are politically or educationally neutral. As we increase our understanding of the impact of the stories we tell and the agendas we promote on students' success, we also increase our obligation to help to change the narratives as well as the aims.

Scholars such as Callahan (2005), Guttiérez and Orellana (2006), Kumaravadivelu (2016), and Shapiro (2014) have addressed the myriad ways "nonnative"-speaker MLLs are marginalized and treated as second-class citizens in U.S. educational contexts. From being labeled "Limited English Proficient" (LEP) from the time they begin their English studies, to being positioned as "nonparticipatory" or unable to critically engage with texts (Kumaravadivelu, 2016), English language learners are often socially constructed as less capable than their native-English-speaking peers (Holliday, 2005).

They are often seen as "problems" that need to be dealt with rather than valuable additions to the classroom whose intellectual capacities may be misunderstood if or when educators are not trained to recognize the differences between language barriers and cognitive difficulties (Crumpler et al., 2011; Gutiérrez & Orellana, 2006; Mitchell, 2013). In this way, multilingual learners' educational outcomes are "underwritten by deficit-oriented discourse" that influences teachers' perceptions of their capabilities and thus the quality of instruction they provide to them (Shapiro, 2014, p. 387).

Deficit discourses are closely tied to standardized testing, which has been shown to inadequately showcase MLLs' knowledge and capabilities (Menken, 2008). Despite what educators learn in teacher-preparation programs about the value of student-centered learning and "meeting students where they are," when faced with daily pressures of meeting performance standards and testing outcomes, this knowledge often takes a backseat to operating under institutional constraints (Mortenson & Cho, 2018).

Under the "one size fits all" ideology of standardized curricula and testing, teachers may essentialize MLLs and see them as all being the same, which has negative consequences for students' educational outcomes (Bigelow, 2010; Shapiro, 2014). No Child Left Behind (NCLB) ignored years of research regarding English as a Second Language (ESL) education and how to best support linguistically and culturally diverse learners.

Prescriptive curricula that utilize repetition, memorization, and choral reading, combined with a dearth of language specialists in schools, continue to deny MLLs opportunities for dynamic, engaging, and stimulating learning environments (Saavedra & Marx, 2016). A consequence of this lack of understanding and support for MLLs is that these students are often overrepresented in special education programs, as content-area educators may not recognize key distinctions between language barriers and learning disabilities, leading to even greater educational disparities (Taylor, 2006).

"MLLS PLAGIARIZE THEIR WORK"

A common deficit narrative about MLLs is that they all plagiarize their work (Kumaravadivelu, 2003). This view is rooted in a hegemonic mindset that positions the conventions of Western academia surrounding language ownership as being "correct" and the writing traditions and understandings of linguistic ownership of other cultures as being "incorrect" or even "unethical" (Gu & Brooks, 2008). It assumes negative intent on the part of writers who don't use in-text citations, and it positions their writing practices as incompatible with Western academic achievement (Kumaravadivelu, 2016).

This represents an imperialist mindset that subscribes to the view that there is only one way to view both the word and the world; instead, we could be investing thought and class time into creating opportunities for meaningful exchanges of information between people that could result in greater understanding about diverse interpretations of language use and intellectual property, while at the same time teaching students what they need to know to be successful in a Western academic context.

Students from Confucian backgrounds may consider words to be communal property that is passed down from generation to generation (Sowden, 2005), rather than propriety information owned solely by the original author, which is a more individualistic understanding (Chien, 2017; Yang & Lin, 2009). Accidental plagiarism also sometimes occurs due to MLLs' inexperience with writing in the target language (Wheeler, 2009), which can lead to an overreliance on patchwriting (Li & Casanave, 2012).

In order to situate language learners constructively in Western academic contexts and help students succeed, greater and more sensitive consideration for the many cultural and individual factors that may be at play in one instance of plagiarism is needed. While there is of course the need to teach students about plagiarism and academic dishonesty as these concepts are understood in the Western academic world, a more constructive rather than punitive approach is warranted if the end goal is that these students graduate and become contributing, valuable participants to whatever fields they pursue.

Consideration must also be given to the fact that language learners not only are learning a language but also may be internalizing an entirely different cultural system alongside that language. Given this, educators must adopt an approach of patience, openness, and willingness to educate students on the finer points of these differences.

This may necessitate a reexamination of harsh penalties surrounding academic integrity at educational institutions, integrating more explicit instruction on citation styles and formatting across disciplines, as well as educating teachers about the writing traditions of the language learners with whom they may come into contact so that teachers can understand both the ideas and practices students may be coming into their classrooms with, as well as how to help them succeed in a Western academic context.

INSTITUTIONAL LABELS, CLASSROOM MARGINALIZATION, AND EDUCATIONAL OUTCOMES

Beyond the assimilation agendas and deficit narratives about MLLs that circulate in schools, Saavedra and Marx (2016) have discussed the additional surveillance, marginalization, and regulation of these students that are baked into the K–12 curriculum. Linguistically minoritized children are exposed to discourses of control that devalue their home language use and position them as lacking if they use their home language in the classroom (Saavedra & Marx, 2016). Schools communicate to MLLs that their home languages (and the cultures that go along with them) are not valuable or welcome in the classroom through English-only policies that govern school settings implicitly or explicitly (Chen, 2020; Menken & Solorza, 2014).

Furthermore, classifications like "Limited English Proficient" (LEP), "Students with Interrupted/Inconsistent Formal Education" (SIFE), and "Long-Term English Learner" (LTEL) all have an impact on how teachers see students as well as on how students see themselves (Boldt, 2001). The impact of these positionings has lasting consequences that can strengthen societal stratifications already in existence (p. 102).

MLLs' positioning as outsiders is relayed not only through stories communicated by institutional labels and among stories told by educators but also through their physical placement in schools. TESOL teachers' rooms are often located far away from the center of the school and are sometimes even put in a separate annex (Clemente & Collison, 2000). When MLLs are included in the regular education classroom, it is not uncommon for them to be in the back of the room working individually with a language specialist rather than integrated with the rest of the class (Saavedra & Marx, 2016).

Researchers have also found that this one-on-one instruction may not even occur, depending on the resources the school has, which may result in the language learner not only being separated from their peers but also missing out on valuable content with nothing replacing it (Saavedra & Marx, 2016).

This lack of content knowledge and inadequate preparation has long-term effects on MLLs' success in K–12 settings. For example, their high school graduation rates are lower than their native-English-speaking peers, even when controlled for race and class (McFarland et al., 2019). Further, while graduation rates have risen in recent years for White, African American, American Indian, and Hispanic students, these rates have decreased for MLLs (McFarland et al., 2019). In the 2017–2018 school year, for example, the adjusted cohort graduation rate (ACGR) was at an all-time high of 84%, while for students labeled "Limited English Language Proficient," that rate was 66.4% or lower (McFarland et al., 2019).

In addition to having a lower graduation rate than their native-English-speaking peers, as well as a higher dropout rate (McFarland et al., 2019), the achievement gap worsens for MLLs who are not reclassified as being fluent in English until later in their education. According to Shin (2018), students who were classified as an "English language learner" for at least 5 years demonstrated lower academic success and slower English-language proficiency than students who were reclassified as fluent within a 5-year time period.

Students who were not reclassified within this timeframe also demonstrated lower attendance in schools and represented a higher proportionality of students needing special education services (Shin, 2018), although this does not necessarily mean all of these students had a learning disability since, as addressed above, language difficulties and learning disabilities are often conflated in K–12 education (Sanatullova-Allison & Robison-Young, 2016).

Exacerbating the issues of inadequate services as well as misdiagnoses for language learners is the dearth of trained TESOL professionals in the field. During the 2015–2016 school year, for example, the U.S. Department of Education found that 32 states did not have enough teachers (including ESL, bilingual, and dual-language education) for MLLs. A correlated statistic is that only 2% of MLLs are enrolled in gifted education as compared to 7.3% of native-English-speaking students (Sparks & Harwin, 2017).

As can be seen, students' success or failure in school is inextricable from their ethnicity, class, and language (Kena et al., 2014; Noguera & Wing, 2006), as well as the governing narratives and institutional labels that are implicitly or explicitly associated with the institution of education. Furthermore, decreased resource allocation for TESOL services, language learners' overrepresentation in special education programs, their increased dropout rates, and their lower graduation rates are all a testament to an overarching problem that has not been dealt with adequately (Harry & Klingner, 2014).

CHANGING THE NARRATIVE

Evolving the narratives about multilingual learners begins with first acknowledging the harm that has been done both historically and contemporarily to these students. Second, we must identify and acknowledge the many strengths these students bring to our classrooms that may not be adequately tapped into currently and represent a failure on the part of K–12 U.S. schools. Shapiro (2014) has addressed the ways that MLLs themselves have "spoken back" to representations of them that are deficit-based and untrue to their own self-understandings.

Multilingual learners want to be viewed as "intelligent and resourceful" (p. 401), and they do not see themselves reflected in many of the narratives currently told. Gloria Ladson-Billings (2016) has discussed the power of "counternarratives" to disseminate truths that may be overlooked or overshadowed by more powerful "meganarratives" from those with more privilege and access. It is not that these stories don't exist; it is that we haven't been listening to them or providing them a sufficient platform to be heard.

TESOL has a long and complex history in the United States that is intimately woven through with White privilege, settler colonialist ideology, and assimilation agendas (Saavedra & Marx, 2016; Von Esch et al., 2020). The way that MLLs are currently treated in the public education system is a product of that imperialist history, and we cannot understand the everyday instances of racism, xenophobia, and linguicism these students experience without taking a hard look at that past. The coronavirus pandemic of 2020 has brought increased attention to instances of bullying, discrimination, and racism experienced by MLLs in the United States (Hong, 2020; Umansky, 2020).

These instances are not new; they are just being seen now given the political and cultural context of the moment. Further, these incidents require teachers to be vigilant and active in countering false claims about diverse learners—particularly about East Asian students in this particular moment—with truthful, accurate information. Educators have a duty to protect students and ensure that their schooling experiences are ones of safety, constructive knowledge-building, and productive exchanges with others whose traditions and history may be different from theirs.

Instead of continuing to circulate inaccurate and incomplete "single stories" about multilingual learners, educators, administrators, and policymakers can listen to and learn from these students to understand how they see themselves and what we can learn from those self-perceptions about how to more effectively teach them. We must realize that MLLs are valuable members of our classroom, and we must remember that our success as teachers is indivisibly bound with the success of our students. Teachers must be critical of "meganarratives" about MLLs that are based on outdated stereotypes and misinformation. Instead, we must help to circulate new stories that acknowledge the limitless possibilities of all students when they are truly seen and heard.

We must also validate and value students' perspectives, and develop curiosity in ourselves and in our native-English-speaking students about different academic models, languages, and traditions that have existed around the world for centuries and can teach us something about ourselves and the world in which we live. We must also be open-minded and humble enough to challenge our understandings of what is "correct" or "valid" and expand our cultural lenses to accept other academic models as being as rich and meaningful as our own. This humility could result in more authentic cultural exchanges that construct more complex and truer understandings of individuals and societies across cultures.

Finally, teachers must be brave enough to speak out against deficit narratives when we hear them so that more complex, asset-based, and truthful narratives about language learners can emerge. Before we can speak out against these narratives, we need to develop our own awareness of implicit biases that may lay dormant or unknown, since the impact of lifelong societal conditioning is undeniable and can sometimes be so subtle that it goes unnoticed and therefore unchanged (DiAngelo, 2018). If we do not develop this self-awareness, we may not even recognize when we "become like the empire" (Saavedra & Marx, 2016, p. 48) through our behavior and words.

This evolution necessitates personal self-reflection and a need for teacher-education programs to evolve their missions. We must educate future teachers on the racist, xenophobic, and White supremacist foundations of the institution of public schooling in the United States and the discourses of control that serve as a "shadow curriculum" for engendering conformity and obedience into students and citizens (Saavedra & Marx, 2016). Because the majority of K–12 teachers in the United States are White and female (National Center for Education Statistics, 2020), we must also incorporate explicit instruction on implicit bias—for example, through use of the Harvard IAT tests for self-reflection—and incorporate antiracism training into our mission.

Through evolving teacher-preparation programs to more adequately and comprehensively prepare future teachers to work with a diverse student body effectively and sensitively, we can bring our society one step closer to being one that is fair, safe, and welcoming for all.

Freire (2000) wrote that it is "through dialogue, [that] the teacher-of-the-students and the student-of-the-teacher . . . become jointly responsible for a process in which all grow" (p. 80). While it is certainly true that dialogue can lead to greater understanding, to effect change, we must evolve not only the stories we tell but also the actions that follow since a truly decolonial option for changing societal problems will result not from intellectualization of the issues but from tangible actions within our communities (Kumaravadivelu, 2016).

In this case, the most radical action may be to stop talking, and instead listen to the students whose stories have historically been told for them without their consent or input. By listening to MLLs and aligning our actions with greater understanding gleaned from more accurate stories, both past and present, we can evolve our personal and collective stories about one another from those based on misinformation to those that recognize the limitless potential of all of us when we are truthfully seen and heard.

REFERENCES

Bigelow, M. (2010). *Mogadishu on the Mississippi: Language, racialized identity, and education in a new land.* Wiley-Blackwell.

Bittle, A. (2013). I am Asian American. *Education Digest, 79*(4), 57.

Boldt, G. (2001). Failing bodies: Discipline and power in elementary classrooms. *Journal of Curriculum Theorizing, 17*(4), 91–104.

Callahan, R. M. (2005). Tracking and high school English learners: Limiting opportunity to learn. *American Educational Research Journal, 42*(2), 305–328.

Chen, L. (2020). Problematising the English-only policy in EAP: A mixed-methods investigation of Chinese international students' perspectives of academic language policy. *Journal of Multilingual and Multicultural Development, 41*(8), 718–735.

Cheryan, S., & Bodenhausen, G. V. (2000). When positive stereotypes threaten intellectual performance: The psychological hazards of "model minority" status. *Psychological Science, 11*(5), 399–402.

Chien, S.C. (2017). Taiwanese college students' perceptions of plagiarism: Cultural and educational considerations. *Ethics and Behavior, 27*(2), 118–139.

Clemente, R., & Collison, B. B. (2000). The relationships among counselors, ESL teachers, and students. *American School Counselor Association, 3*(5), 339–348.

Crumpler, T. P., Handsfield, L. J., & Dean, T. R. (2011). Constructing difference differently in language and literacy professional development. *Research in the Teaching of English, 46*, 55–91.

Debasish, B. (2010). More than meets the eye. *Language in India, 10*(10), 150–179.

DiAngelo, R. (2018). *White fragility: Why it's so hard for White people to talk about racism.* Beacon Press.

Freire, P. (2000). *Pedagogy of the oppressed* (30th anniversary ed.). Continuum.

Gu, Q., & Brooks, J. (2008). Beyond the accusation of plagiarism. *System, 36*(3), 337–352.

Gutiérrez, K. D., & Orellana, M. F. (2006). The "problem" of English learners: Constructing genres of difference. *Research in the Teaching of English, 40*(4), 502–507.

Harry, B., & Klingner, J. (2014). *Why are so many minority students in special education?: Understanding race and disability in schools* (2nd ed.). Teachers College Press.

Holliday, A. (2005). *The struggle to teach English as an international language.* Oxford University Press.

Hong, A. (2020, March 12). *Amid the coronavirus outbreak, Asian American students like my son face racist taunting. Let's change that.* Chalk Beat. https://www.chalkbeat.org/2020/3/12/21178748/amid-the-coronavirus-outbreak-asian-american-students-like-my-son-face-racist-taunting-let-s-change

Kena, G., Aud, S., Johnson, F., Wang, X., Zhang, J., Rathbun, A., Wilkinson-Flicker, S., Kristapovich, P., Notter, L., Robles-Villalba, V., Nachazel, T., & Dziuba, A. (2014). *The condition of education 2014* (NCES 2014–083). U.S. Department of Education, National Center for Education Statistics. https://nces.ed.gov/pubs2014/2014083.pdf

Kubota, R. (2002). The author responds: (Un)raveling racism in a nice field like TESOL. *TESOL Quarterly, 31*(1), 84–92.

Kumaravadivelu, B. (2003). Problematizing cultural stereotypes in TESOL. *TESOL Quarterly, 37*(4), 709–719.

Kumaravadivelu, B. (2016). The decolonial option in English teaching: Can the subaltern act? *TESOL Quarterly, 50*(1), 66–85.

Kynard, C. (2013). *Vernacular insurrections: Race, Black protest, and the new century in composition-literacies studies.* State University of New York Press.

Ladson-Billings, G. (2016). Just what is critical race theory and what's it doing in a nice field like education? In E. Taylor, D. Gillborn, & G. Ladson-Billings (Eds.), *Foundations of critical race theory in education* (pp. 15–30). Routledge.

Li, Y., & Casanave, C. P. (2012). Two first-year students' strategies for writing from sources: Patchwriting or plagiarism? *Journal of Second Language Writing, 21*(2), 165–180.

McBee Orzulak, M. J. (2015). Disinviting deficit ideologies: Beyond "that's standard," "that's racist," and "that's your mother tongue." *Research in the Teaching of English, 50*(2), 176–198.

McFarland, J., Cui, J., Holmes, J., & Wang, X. (2019). *Trends in high school dropout and completion rates in the United States: 2019.* U.S. Department of Education, National Center for Education Statistics. https://nces.ed.gov/pubs2020/2020117.pdf

Menken, K. (2008). *English learners left behind: Standardized testing as language policy.* Multilingual Matters.

Menken, K., & Solorza, C. (2014). No child left bilingual: Accountability and the elimination of bilingual education programs in New York City schools. *Educational Policy, 28*(1), 96–125.

Mitchell, K. (2013). Race, difference, meritocracy, and English: Majoritarian stories in the education of secondary multilingual learners. *Race Ethnicity and Education, 16*, 339–364.

Morris, M. W. (2016). *Pushout: The criminalization of Black girls in schools.* The New Press.

Mortenson, L., & Cho, H. (2018). English language teachers as policymakers and advocates for displaced students in the era of accountability. In K. M. Harrison, M. Sadiku, & F. V. Tochon, *Displacement planet Earth: Plurilingual education and identity for 21st-century schools.* Deep University Press.

National Center for Education Statistics. (2020, May). *Characteristics of public school teachers.* https://nces.ed.gov/programs/coe/indicator_clr.asp

Noguera, P., & Wing, J. Y. (Eds.). (2006). *Unfinished business: Closing the racial achievement gap in our schools.* Jossey-Bass.

Saavedra, C. M., & Marx, S. (2016). School as taming wild tongues and bodies. *Global Studies of Childhood, 6*(1), 42–52.

Sanatullova-Allison, E., & Robison-Young, V. A. (2016). Overrepresentation: An overview of the issues surrounding the identification of English language learners with learning disabilities. *International Journal of Special Education, 31*(2), 1–13.

Shapiro, S. (2014). "Words that you said got bigger": English Language Learners' lived experiences of deficit discourse. *Research in the Teaching of English, 48*(4), 386–406.

Shin, N. (2018). The effects of the initial English Language Learner classification on students' later academic outcomes. *Educational Evaluation and Policy Analysis, 40*(2), 175–195. https://doi.org/10.3102/0162373717737378

Sowden, C. (2005). Plagiarism and the culture of multilingual students in higher education abroad. *ELT Journal, 59*, 226–233.

Sparks, S. D., & Harwin, A. (2017, June 21). Too few ELLs land in gifted classes. *Education Week.* https://www.edweek.org/ew/articles/2017/06/21/too-few-ELL-students-land-in-gifted.html

Tatum, B. D. (2017). *Why are all the Black kids sitting together in the cafeteria?: And other conversations about race* (20th anniversary ed.). Basic Books.

Taylor, L. (2006). Wrestling with race: The implications of integrative antiracism education for immigrant ESL youth. *TESOL Quarterly, 40*, 519–544.

Umansky, I. (2020, June 9). *COVID-19's impact on English learner students.* Policy Analysis for California Education. https://edpolicyinca.org/newsroom/covid-19s-impact-english-learner-students

Von Esch, K. S., Motha, S., & Kobota, R. (2020). Race and language teaching. *Language Teaching, 53*, 391–421.

Wheeler, G. (2009). Plagiarism in the Japanese universities: Truly a cultural matter? *Journal of Second Language Writing, 8*(1), 17–29.

Yang, M., & Lin, S. (2009, September 28–30). *The perception of referencing and plagiarism amongst students coming from Confucian heritage cultures* [Conference presentation]. Asia Pacific Conference on Educational Integrity (4APCEI), NSW Australia.

Chapter 5

English Language Bilingualism

Judith A. Orth and Kathleen M. Hargiss

In today's public schools, there are many ESL students. Their native languages range from Spanish to Russian to Niger-Congo. Many educators believe that ESL students are easy to recognize in a classroom. This population consists of students who enter our classrooms without speaking one word of English.

Bilingualism is a phenomenon that is seen worldwide and is also very prevalent in the United States. It was recently estimated that 21.6% of all individuals in the United States speak another language (i.e., other than English) in the home (U.S. Census Bureau, 2021). Of this, Latinos are the largest culturally and linguistically diverse population in the United States, estimated to be 18.5% of the total U.S. population (U.S. Census Bureau, 2021).

However pervasive bilingualism may be in the United States, many misperceptions continue to exist regarding the nature of bilingualism and working with bilingual students, especially when assessing their language and learning abilities. Bilingualism is a "complex linguistic, cognitive, and social phenomena" (Brice et al., 2006, p. 45).

Many times, these students enter the classroom, fearful of how they will be received by their fellow classmates. They have sweaty palms and are not really understanding the expectations in front of them. In the interim, these students remain uncomfortably silent in class as they are attempting to adjust to a new school environment. The only comfort these students experience in their new classroom is when they have a native-language classmate to interact with verbally.

This period of silence demonstrated by the English Language Learner (ELL) student may last for a few days to several months. This discomfort is experienced not only by the student but also by the teacher assigned to teach the ESL student. It is a double-edged sword for the student and the teacher. The student does not understand the expectations regarding how to act behaviorally, how to make new friends, or how to achieve academic success. The teacher is also frustrated, for student responses occur seldom or not at all (Robinson et al., n.d.).

The question the teacher needs to address is how a second language is acquired for their student(s). Students exhibit a variety of patterns illustrating rates and styles of acquisition. Without specific training on how to teach an ELL student, the teacher is often in the dark on how to answer the above question. On the ELL student's exposure to English, there can be a deep crevasse in their learning curve of the English language. Are they exposed to English at home in conversations with their parents and other family members? Do they watch television in their native language or English? Some students adapt immediately to a new language, and others struggle for months or years in acquiring a command of this second language (Au, 2011).

When dealing with ELL students, there are many components to address before the student begins to learn new English words: for example, motivation, type of personality, attitudes, and learning styles of each student. Students classified as extrovert personalities are seen to attempt increased verbal interactions with their teacher and classmates. The introverted students appear to experience difficulties as they are unable to respond to their counterparts or remain in a world of silence. What is also critical when teaching an ELL student is how the student reacts to the instructional style of the teacher. Finally, is the student able to practice their new language acquisition with others, outside of school (Au, 2011)?

As previously noted, not all ELL students come to the learning arena with confidence and acceptance of the challenges afforded. Not all students enter the new classroom using the language spoken at home. Some of these students come from homes where multiple languages are spoken, which complicates the learning of English even more. These learners, many times, have not established a primary language, which increases the difficulties in developing a new language.

These types of learners are sometimes classified as learning disabled, a label that should not be placed on any student without sufficient medical documentation. However, as educators, we know that often, labels are unjustly placed on students, and those labels follow the students through their entire public education. When working with ELL students, it is imperative that teachers explore each student's academic and personal history. Without having a true understanding of their ELL student, teachers will not be able to guide their student's transition from their native language to their second or third language—English (Au, 2011).

English Language Learners come to school with a wide variety of background knowledge, language, and literacy skills. The schooling experience of ELLs is impacted by many factors such as time in school, quality of instruction, transiency, home environment, and past emotional experiences in school. The following vignettes illustrate some of these differences (Au, 2011).

ELL PROFICIENCY STAGES

Stage 1

ELL students at this stage have very limited or no understanding of English. These learners never use English to communicate with their peers. This type of learner can respond nonverbally to commands, statements, and questions in simple forms. In time, when the learner's oral comprehension increases, they are seen using simple words and phrases, and surprisingly may use English spontaneously.

It is important to note that the ELL student should be developing Basic Interpersonal Communication Skills (BICS). They

- have an increased understanding of basic spoken English, which is accomplished by observations during instruction;
- communicate nonverbally in response to questions, statements, or basic commands;
- respond in simple form to questions, statements, and commands;
- attempt to repeat language through individual words or simple phrases; and
- acquire a level of limited English reading comprehension.

This type of information is associated with day-to-day common language needed to be able to interact in social situations. A few examples relate to being able to communicate: talking on the phone, playing sports, or attending parties with their peers.

Stage 2

At this point in the learning process, ELL students at this stage can comprehend and understand simple topics. The learners can converse in short conversations relying on nonverbal cues, gestures, and repetition. Common and frequent errors are seen at this stage. ELLs in stage 2

- observe peers before trying to complete a task;
- respond using basic words and expressions;
- communicate using memorized simple phrases;

- rely on nonverbal communication and familiarity;
- memorize simple phrases;
- exhibit some reading behaviors; and
- demonstrate self-corrections. (Alberta Benchmarks, 2010)

Stage 3

ELL students in this stage can understand standard speech delivered in most settings along with some repetition. This type of learner can communicate orally in most settings. At this stage, the learner can comprehend the content of many texts independently, although they may not qualify to be on a specific grade level. Most learners now will be able to basically read and write. These students

- comprehend newly found words in the first language and then translate into English;
- experience problems with grammar and tenses;
- interact occasionally in conversations and class discussions related to familiar topics; and
- produce longer phrases and complete sentences. (Alberta Benchmarks, 2010)

Stage 4

ELL students at this stage have basic-proficient language skills for day-to-day communications. This learner may still have trouble with idiomatic expressions and words with more than one meaning. At this juncture in time, this type of learner can communicate in new or unfamiliar settings. These learners can write for personal and academic purposes, though it is still possible for errors to occur. Students in this stage

- engage in conversations;
- rehearse words and phrases in the first language, and then translate into English;
- partake in class discussions;
- accept assistance in improving the language proficiency; and
- are able to use more complex sentences and phrases. (Alberta Benchmarks, 2010)

Stage 5

ELLs at this advanced stage will have demonstrated English proficiency as determined by state assessment instruments (ELPA—English Language Proficient Assessment). These learners are expected to be able to participate fully with grade-level peers. They are able to

- use language comparable to a native speaker;
- listen, read, write, and speak in the English language;
- lose the first language and not rely on translation to the second language; and
- use assistive technology and various translation tools. (Alberta Benchmarks, 2010)

LANGUAGE 1 VERSUS LANGUAGE 2

ELL students know two languages. They have their native language, which is referred to as Language 1. The new language they are learning is referred to as Language 2. Each has language specific identifiers for an ELL student and some identifiers are in both Language 1 and Language 2. Below are the identifiers for Language 1 and Language 2 and the overlapping identifiers for Language 1 and Language 2. Below, according to Ipek (2009), are the comparing and contrasting first and second language acquisitions one has to experience when learning a new language.

Language 1 (Native language)

- Students are normally fluent in their native language
- ELL students demonstrate language competence in their native language
- Instruction of Language 1 is not often necessary
- Not much correction is needed in their native language when writing or speaking
- Social factors are understood and adhered to in Language 1.

Language 2 (New language student is acquiring)

- The older the person, the less likely they will achieve mastery of the new language
- Due to the variation of learning styles, acquiring a new language may be a challenge that proves too difficult

- Many times, when learning a new language, the learner will backslide to their earlier stages of language development
- Instruction from a person who speaks the second language, is necessary and helpful
- When learning a second language, the student is usually unable to form complete grammatical judgments
- Since most learners are visual learners, it is especially helpful to include pictures when learning a new language
- Social factors must be learned for Language 2.

Overlapping of Language 1 and Language 2

- When teaching a new language, each student has a different starting point. Therefore, begin at the basic stages of language development to determine where you need to begin teaching Language 2 to the student
- The depth of knowledge is beyond the level of input. This, too, is different for every student and must be determined when you begin teaching the new language to the student
- The acquisition order of the new language must be determined, and this can be achieved through language assessments of the new language
- Behavioristic views of the acquisition order (Ipek, 2009)
- There are three stages of the Zone of Proximal Development (ZPD). The teacher must determine the ZPD stage of each student who is learning the second language,
  - Zone 1—Tasks outside of the student's ZPD are those that are unable to be completed, even with the help of an expert.
  - Zone 2—Tasks a student can accomplish with assistance.
  - Zone 3—Tasks a students can accomplish without assistance (Meyers, 2005).
- Teachers need to give equal attention to students learning Language 1 and Language 2 (Ipek, 2009).

LEARNING STYLES

A learning style is how the brain processes a task and new information. A learning style is an automatic cognitive process rather than a conscious choice (Carver & Orth, 2017). There are three cognitive learning styles for all learners: visual, auditory, and kinesthetic.

- Visual: Visual learners must "see" what they are learning, through written text, pictures, maps, graphs, flashcards, charts, etc. This type of learner must "see" information to process it.
- Auditory: Auditory learners must "hear" the information that they are learning in order to cognitively process it. This entails speaking and listening. Many times, an auditory learner may find pictures or the written text challenging, for this is not how they cognitively process information.
- Kinesthetic: To cognitively process information, this type of learner learns through sensations and movements of the body. The students learn through physical activities or anything that includes physical motion. Manipulation of items or touching materials is also part of this learning style.

To teach ELL students, it is imperative to incorporate all learning styles into classroom lessons. By doing so, you will know that you are meeting your students' learning style needs (Carver & Orth, 2017).

English-language bilingualism has become more normal in today's public-school classrooms. Students from all over the world are matriculating into classrooms where previously only English had been the main spoken language. It is imperative for today's teachers to understand how to teach ELL students and determine their specific needs. This chapter discusses how to teach ELL students in the classroom, examples of what ELL students experience in a classroom where English is spoken, the stages of ELL proficiencies, a language 1 versus language 2 Venn Diagram, and a description of learning styles of all students (including ELLs) (Walki, 1996).

REFERENCES

Alberta Benchmarks. (2010). Supporting English Language Learners' benchmarks in Alberta K–12. In *English Language Learners—ELL Proficiency Levels*. Calgary Board of Education.

Au, K. (2011). *Literacy achievement and diversity*. Teachers College Press.

Brice, A., Kester, E. & Brice, R. (2006). *English language learner characteristics: An overview of assessment issues*. https://www.pediastaff.com/slp/english-language-learner-characteristics-an-overview-of-assessment-issues-5338

Carver, L., & Orth, J. (2017). *Coach*. Rowman & Littlefield.

Ipek, H. (2009*)*. Comparing and contrasting first and second language acquisition: Implications for language teachers. *English Language Teaching, 2*(2), 155–163.

Meyers, D. G. (2005). *Exploring psychology. Sixth edition*. Worth Publishers.

Robinson, N., Keogh, B., & Kusuma-Powell, O. (n.d.). Who are ESL students? In Overseas Schools Advisory Council (Ed.), *Count me in: Developing inclusive international schools* (chapter 6). U.S. Department of State. https://2009-2017.state.gov/m/a/os/44038.htm

U.S. Census Bureau. (2021). *Quick facts* [data table]. https://www.census.gov/quickfacts/fact/table/US#

Walki, A. (1996). *Access and engagement: Program design and instructional approaches for immigrant students in secondary school.* Center for Applied Linguistics.

Chapter 6

Positioning English Language Learners for Mathematical Success

Erin Smith

Many of us have experienced sitting in a meeting, class, or other event and felt reluctant to speak. We may have felt like an outsider or didn't belong, or thought we weren't valued, needed, or appreciated. In such situations, we may feel anxious, fearful, frustrated, confused, nervous, or hurt. Any of these feelings can lead us to turn in, pull back, or shut down. Unfortunately, these feelings are not unique to adults; they are experienced by children as well.

English Language Learners (ELLs) may experience such feelings in school settings, which can prevent them from participating in classroom discussions or even speaking with their teacher. This is particularly troublesome in mathematics classrooms because ELLs learn mathematics alongside English as they participate in discussions (Lightbrown & Spada, 2013; Moschkovich, 2002; National Council of Teachers of Mathematics, 2014). If ELLs don't feel valued or that they belong in the mathematics classroom, they are unlikely to participate in discussions, and their mathematical learning will suffer. How do teachers ensure ELLs feel valued in their classroom and possess ideas worth sharing? It all comes down to positioning.

THE IMPORTANCE OF POSITIONS AND POSITIONING

Every day teachers say a variety of things to students in mathematics classrooms, such as "Great job," "She was being very efficient," and "That's right." These statements are examples of a teacher assigning a position to a student. A *position* can determine the social expectations and what people can do and say in a given situation (Harré & van Langenhove, 1991; van

Langenhove, 2011). Positions are also relational (i.e., tied to one another) and dynamic.

Positions are important because they can determine how students participate in the classroom (van Langenhove & Harré, 1999). Take, for instance, a teacher who says, "Hari, you're not good at math." With this statement, the teacher positions Hari as mathematically incompetent. In return, Hari may feel hurt, angry, frustrated, or scorned and will be unlikely to participate or try in the future. The feelings Hari has may be amplified because the statement was said by the teacher—the content "expert" and authority figure.

Although the example of Hari is very clear, teachers can also position students in other, more subtle ways through their words and actions. For instance, teachers of ELLs have been found to never call on ELLs to share their thinking, place ELLs at the remediation table, cut ELLs off, or say things like "How can we slow this down for John?" Over time, these words and actions can be just as impactful to students as overt statements—like the one made to Hari—are, and unfortunately, these positions are all too common for ELLs.

Although some people may think, "Well, I just won't position students," this is impossible. Positioning happens all the time, in *every* interaction, and cannot be avoided. It happens in face-to-face interactions, on the phone, in email, through books, and so on. It's not a matter of *not positioning* students, but *how to position* students, particularly ELLs, so they can be mathematically successful.

HOW TO POSITION ELLS FOR MATHEMATICAL SUCCESS

1. Establish Goals

Effective teachers of ELLs create short- and long-term goals for *each* ELL in their class at the start of the school year and continually update them. These goals are connected to mathematical learning, language learning, participation, and socioemotional development and drive what teachers do and say in the classroom.

Mathematical learning goals should be focused; be tied to the learning objectives of the lesson, unit, or course; and foster practices required for success. For example, one teacher identified the following mathematical goals:

> I want her to have strong mathematical thinking without just having to rely on a set of rules. I want her to be able to approach problems and be able to think

of lots of different ways to solve a problem. I want her to select strategies that are efficient.

This teacher's goals identified a desire to increase the ELL's flexibility in mathematical thinking, increase mathematical reasoning, and reduce reliance on algorithms. Mathematical goals should attend strictly to the ELL's mathematical thinking and learning, not other aspects that fall under language learning goals, such as language.

Language learning goals are important for ELLs since ELLs learn English alongside mathematics. Goals such as "I want him to share his strategy orally at the board" or "I want her to use complete sentences when writing mathematical justifications" focus on the language needed to be mathematically successful. Teachers who construct language learning goals for ELLs are better attuned to the language demands of the lesson and mathematics in general and are better situated to facilitate language learning. Moreover, these teachers recognize they are responsible for fostering language development and don't offload all this work onto others.

Participation goals are important for ELLs since they are often left to sit on the sidelines in mathematics classes. To prevent this from happening in their own classrooms, effective teachers create goals for participation. For example, "I want Qadhri to raise his hand at least once every lesson." Another teacher's goal was "I try to get her to participate in some capacity in every lesson." This goal is notable because the teacher sought the student's participation in *every* mathematics lesson, which provided varied opportunities for the student to share her mathematical thinking *and* develop language.

Socioemotional development goals are also important for ELLs to ensure they feel welcomed and valued in the classroom. For example, one teacher created the following goal for a new student: "I want him to develop productive relationships with at least two peers in the class." When ELLs feel valued and welcomed in the classroom, they are more likely to feel comfortable sharing their mathematical thinking, as one teacher noticed: "Before she had met some friends, she was kind of reluctant to participate, but now she is one of the first hands up a lot of times and wanting to get up and participate."

Once mathematics, language, participation, and socioemotional development goals are created, effective teachers identify actionable steps they will take in the classroom to ensure each ELL can meet their goals and position them for mathematical success.

2. Share Thinking

ELLs, just like other students, must participate in mathematical discussions if they are to learn (National Council of Teachers of Mathematics, 2014). To ensure ELLs can and want to participate, effective teachers position ELLs as active members in the classroom who possess ideas worthy of sharing. One way effective teachers do this is to ask ELLs to share their mathematical thinking during class discussions. This can be as simple as asking, "How did you figure that out?" "Why would that be ___?" or "What's similar about these two strategies?" Such questions position ELLs as mathematically competent, facilitate their participation, and advance language learning.

Although some people may think ELLs must be proficient in English before participating in mathematical discussions, effective teachers do not put ELLs' mathematical learning on hold as they learn English. Instead, they recognize this happens alongside mathematical learning.

3. Present Important Mathematical Ideas at the Board

When ELLs are invited to take up this space at the front of the classroom, which is typically reserved for the teacher, they are *physically* positioned as the teacher. When ELLs demonstrate important mathematical ideas to peers, they are *metaphorically* positioned as the teacher.

Effective teachers take advantage of both of these physical and metaphorical positions to position ELLs. For example, effective teachers have ELLs present their problem-solving strategies at the board, which positions ELLs as possessing important mathematical ideas and as students who can explain their thinking to others, can be learned from, and are active participants in the classroom. In addition to the mathematical benefits of sharing problem-solving strategies, ELLs benefit from varied use of language for extended periods of time—a necessity for proficiency.

While some teachers may be scared an ELL will be uncomfortable presenting important mathematical ideas at the board, effective teachers do not let their own fear restrict ELLs' mathematical success. Instead, they may use images or scanned work that ELLs can gesture to as they talk to aid their presentation. Alternatively, they prepare an ELL to present by telling them in advance or giving them time to rehearse.

Effective teachers also create spaces where making mathematical mistakes is normal and part of the learning process. So, if an ELL makes a mistake while presenting, it doesn't negate their mathematical ideas or position in the classroom. Most importantly, effective teachers have ELLs present important mathematical ideas at the board in the *first week* of the school and continue it throughout the year.

4. Attend to Peers' Thinking

Being able to question, critique, and restate the reasoning of others are important mathematical practices. However, all too often, ELLs aren't asked to do these. Effective teachers ask ELLs to comment on or question a peer's thinking (e.g., "Samuel, why would people be going 'no'?") or restate it (e.g., "Lea, can you go up there [to the board] and explain what Emily did?"). This positions ELLs as students who attend to and can explain the mathematical thinking of others.

Effective teachers also ask peers to comment on an ELL's thinking. For instance, after an ELL presented their problem-solving strategy, a teacher asked, "Questions, comments, or compliments for Bruno about his strategy?" Prompts like this reinforce expectations that peers attend to *everyone's* mathematical thinking, position the ELL's ideas as worthy of further consideration, retain the ELL's thinking at the center of the conversation, and provide opportunities for peers to critique, elaborate on, or compliment the mathematical thinking of others.

Effective teachers also allow ELLs to moderate this discussion by fielding questions—an act often reserved for the teacher. Yet, for this to occur, effective teachers spend time at the beginning of the school year to teach their students how to question, offer compliments, and challenge each other's thinking in respectful ways. For instance, effective teachers post anchor charts of acceptable things to say or do, provide students with bookmarks to reference if they're unsure what to say, role play or model interactions with body language, and explicitly discuss respectful and disrespectful ways of interacting with peers in mathematics.

5. Possess Valued Ways of Thinking and Acting

Teachers often evaluate students' mathematical thinking through statements such as "Really cool idea," "Really smart strategies," or "Nice job." These types of evaluations are important for ELLs when they are used *before* they share to set the stage. For example, a teacher could say "Zora had a *really cool idea*. Can you explain your idea?" "I saw *really smart* strategies on number 1. Chintan, can you explain what you did?" or "I scanned in Alfredia's work because she did a *nice job* of explaining this a few different ways." When evaluative statements are used to preface ELLs' talk, they are publicly distinguished from peers and positioned as students who have valued ways of thinking that everyone can learn from and should hear. Moreover, such statements can bolster ELLs' confidence and reduce feelings of discomfort or hesitancy when sharing.

Effective teachers also explicitly call attention to the valued ways ELLs engage in mathematics. For instance, a teacher may draw explicit attention to the efficiency of an ELL's strategy by stating, "Zainab was being very efficient," or recommend peers embody aspects of an ELL, such as "If you wanted to be more efficient, you might think about it like Mariam did." When ELLs are positioned as acting in mathematically valued ways, they are positioned as mathematically competent. Moreover, statements like these can counter stereotypes that ELLs are often in need of remediation in mathematics.

ENSURING ELLS ACHIEVE IN MATHEMATICS

Some people may think, "Well, shouldn't I position every student for mathematical success?" and the answer is *yes*. Unfortunately, this is not the reality in many U.S. mathematics classrooms, and ELLs' mathematical learning has suffered as a result. Moreover, since ELLs represent one of the fastest-growing demographics in U.S. public schools, it is now more important than ever for teachers to understand how to position ELLs for mathematical success.

REFERENCES

Harré, R., & van Langenhove, L. (1991). Varieties of positioning. *Journal for the Theory of Social Behaviour, 21*, 393–407.

Lightbrown, P. M., & Spada, N. (2013). *How languages are learned* (4th ed.). Oxford University Press.

Moschkovich, J. (2002). A situated and sociocultural perspective on bilingual mathematics learners. *Mathematical Thinking and Learning, 4*, 189–212.

National Council of Teachers of Mathematics. (2014). *Principles to action: Ensuring mathematical success for all*. Author.

van Langenhove, L. (2011). Conversation as the primary social reality. In L. van Langenhove (Ed.), *People and societies: Rom Harré and designing the social sciences* (pp. 65–68). Routledge.

van Langenhove, L., & Harré, R. (1999). Introducing positioning theory. In R. Harré & L. van Langenhove (Eds.), *Positioning theory: Moral contexts of intentional action* (pp. 14–31). Blackwell.

Chapter 7

Educational Journeys

Youth Voices as the Impetus for Social Justice Curriculum in Latinx Multilingual Classrooms

Rubén A. González

Latinx youth comprise 77% of all students identified as "English learners" in K–12 schools in the United States (McFarland et al., 2018). The "English Language Learner" (ELL) label often results in Latinx multilingual students being placed in support courses, such as SDAIE (Specifically Designed Academic Instruction in English), intended to provide access to core content curriculum and academic language support (Genzuk, 2011).

Yet, as Umansky (2018) concluded, the ELL label also triggers negative changes in a student's school experiences. In particular, students with the ELL label are tracked into classrooms where teachers hold low expectations of them (Gutierrez & Orellana, 2006) and where students are taught in a manner that is diminished, slower-paced, and lacking academic rigor (Dabach, 2014).

In addition, not only are Latinx multilingual students tracked into classrooms where teachers hold low expectations of them and where teachers foster confining learning environments, but also students rarely see themselves reflected in the classroom curriculum (Valenzuela, 1999). Also, within the larger sociopolitical climate of the United States, Martinez and colleagues (2019) posit Latinx multilingual youth have their school experiences shaped by narratives of being "criminals, rapists, gang members, uneducated, and so forth" (p. 452).

Such a negative school experience for Latinx multilingual youth is exacerbated by the fact that many teachers feel ill-equipped to address the sociopolitical issues affecting minoritized youth (Garcia & Dutro, 2018). In short, the ELL label results in negative school experiences for Latinx multilingual students in the areas of academic development and social emotional well-being in K–12 schools.

As a result of this current educational context for Latinx multilingual students, this chapter focuses on two distinct ways teachers can work with Latinx multilingual youth to co-construct classroom curricula that create more humane and critical learning environments. First, how can teachers center student experiences to create a classroom community in which students, individually and collectively, are able to name, analyze, and refute the forms of oppression they endure in educational and social settings?

Second, how can teachers use this classroom community and learning environment to create a curriculum grounded in the lived experiences of students that is both responsive to their experiences and academically rigorous? One way to work toward these two goals is for teachers to employ Educational Journeys (Annamma, 2016; Rodríguez, 2018) in K–12 classrooms as a pedagogical and curricular approach.

FLIPPING THE MIRROR AND STARTING WITH THE SELF

Students create their Educational Journeys based on pivotal and (dis)empowering academic and social lived experiences, and share their experiences through a visual narrative of images and/or words (González, 2018). The cultural narratives students share are rooted in a critical sociopolitical analysis, specifically a critical racial, social, and political understanding and critique of their lived experiences. Through the use of Educational Journeys, students draw on and validate their lived experiences, and provide a learning environment and curriculum in which they analyze and critique social issues that affect them, their communities, and others. Examples from this study include students discussing issues of race and racism, sexism, socioeconomic status, and immigration, among others. Students also employed the use of photography along with colorful illustrations and the use of words to depict their schooling experiences.

The Educational Journey process and activity allows students to draw on their own cultural frameworks and lived experiences to illuminate and disrupt existing power relations as they (re)shape and (re)imagine their identities in transformative ways (Camangian, 2010). Students then co-create learning environments and curricula in which they can "heal, build, and thrive, and to imagine a new social condition for and with historically marginalized communities" (Rodríguez, 2018, p. 216). Such a learning environment and curriculum provide minoritized students with the opportunity to develop knowledge of the self while recognizing, refuting, and healing from various forms of social oppression in their everyday lives.

As co-constructors of knowledge with one another, students foster a mutual understanding of difficult past and present life experiences, craft a hopeful future, and see beyond the perceived differences they experience in various social contexts (Camangian, 2010; Rodríguez, 2018). Students draw connections between their respective cultural and social lived experiences to foster more positive and caring relationships, creating a classroom community where they begin to (re)imagine and (re)shape their individual and collective identities.

In creating such a classroom community, students foster a transformative and academically rigorous learning environment. As Howard (2001) discovered, an investment in creating caring and healing classroom environments, where student lived experiences are the primary point of curricular departure, fosters an optimal learning environment.

While the creating and sharing of Educational Journeys can be perceived as less of an academic task and more of a strategy for healing (Ginwright, 2010), this fails to realize how helping students heal from various forms of oppression fosters the conditions for a classroom community conducive to transformational learning. In particular, as posited by Duncan-Andrade (2009), teachers must use the classroom environment grounded in the individual and collective healing of students as a bridge to more academically rigorous learning, and "bust the false binary that suggest [teachers] must choose between an academically rigorous pedagogy and one geared toward [healing]" (p. 186). As such, Educational Journeys are not limited to solely tapping into the emotions of students, but serve as a bridge from the personal to the academically rigorous and vice versa—a cyclical approach to socioemotional and academic development.

SETTING

This study was conducted in a ninth-grade English SDAIE course, composed almost entirely of Latinx multilingual youth, during the 2013–2014 school year in a high school in northern California. The student-identified themes within Educational Journeys became the basis for subsequent lessons and units. The themes were integrated into the mandated classroom curriculum and adhered to the Common Core State Standards (CCSS), reinforcing content knowledge and academic skills through student-centered, critical, and humane approaches.

THE SHARING OF ONE'S SOUL

To model vulnerability and to not ask students to engage in sharing possibly traumatic experiences without being willing to do the same, the teacher first shared their Educational Journey with students. The teacher focused their Educational Journey on sharing social and academic experiences in various contexts, such as navigating school and larger social settings as the child of immigrants, being pushed out of high school, and being the first person in their family to attend college. The focus of their Educational Journey was to demonstrate how different components of one's life are not siloed.

Moments of both triumphs and difficulties were shared, as to not foster a space of only sharing negative experiences and trafficking in damage centered narratives (Tuck, 2009), but to lead with possibility instead of problems (Warren, 2021). The following day, students created and began to share their Educational Journeys. Over the course of two class periods, students shared their Educational Journeys as everyone sat in a circle, each student projecting their visual representation as they addressed the class. Students then had an informal dialogue with one another after each presentation, identifying, discussing, and analyzing recurring and/or new themes that were evoked during the Educational Journeys.

FOSTERING A POSITIVE CLASSROOM COMMUNITY

The teacher presenting their Educational Journey signaled to students an opportunity to "speak their truth" and validated the sharing of personal experiences as an academic endeavor. Students fostered a classroom space rooted in a strong foundation of community among one another through the sharing of communal struggles in educational and social settings. Students realized they were individuals, and a collective, able to overcome various forms of internal, interpersonal, and institutional oppression in multiple educational and larger social settings. As students built positive bonds with one another, they realized they were "not alone" in their struggles and the difficulties they endured were part of larger systems of oppression affecting them and their communities.

Discovering these common struggles allowed students to become more comfortable in class and among their peers. Marco demonstrated this increased comfort, explaining, "I feel safe that I can say whatever I want [in class] without being judged or made fun of. . . . When [classmates] cried, I just wanted to cry with them because I felt a connection to them." The connection between students allowed them to be their genuine selves with one another and to more deeply explore their lived experiences—free from judgment of others and their own self-imposed, internalized gaze.

This increased level of comfort in class not only influenced a student's individual sense of self but also influenced the students collectively in the fostering of a stronger classroom community. Students no longer "othered" one another and moved beyond some of the negative perceptions they held toward each other earlier in the school year (e.g., evoking sexist, homophobic, and ableist language). This was revealed in Rocío's reflection of how Educational Journeys helped foster a stronger classroom community:

> Educational Journeys helped us not judge each other. You know what [classmates] have been through and see you have similar stories. . . . You think about how other people are affected [by negative experiences] in their lives instead of just thinking about yourself. . . . You hear people speak. You cry, laugh, and feel you know them better. You feel more connected to them—you see yourself in them.

The sharing of Educational Journeys had a profound influence on students individually and collectively. Students had a more positive sense of self in being able to share their lived educational and social experiences. This stronger sense of self allowed students to be more comfortable in class and helped them to find similarities beyond their perceived differences. Students developed a sense of belonging among each other, which helped foster a closer and more caring classroom community through the reflection, sharing, and listening of lived experiences via Educational Journeys.

In addition, such a classroom community allowed students to engage in a much deeper and critical analysis of their individual and shared lived experiences. Most importantly, students began to analyze their lived experiences in different contexts, as prevalent themes from their Educational Journeys were integrated into the mandated classroom curriculum throughout the school year.

DEVELOPING A CRITICAL SOCIOPOLITICAL ANALYSIS

As students reflected on their lived experiences, they analyzed the root causes of issues they identified. They moved toward critically analyzing their experiences, rather than simply (re)telling experiences solely based on emotion. Students were able to develop the skill to read situations in their daily lives and to differentiate between root causes (e.g., institutional racism) and symptoms of oppression (e.g., racially disproportionate school suspension rates).

Students began to name their experiences and offer analysis and critique of how these moments affected them and others, and how these experiences influenced their past, present, and future lives.

Leo was an example of the paradigm shift from individualized experiences focused on symptoms of oppression, to a more systematic reading of situations in which the root causes of oppression were analyzed:

> You see that word [points to the word *bitch*, which is crossed out]? I don't say that word. You'll never hear it from me. I used to sit in my room as a little kid—8 years old. My parents would be in the next room, and I would hear that word when my dad would yell at my mom and beat her. This happened all the time.

Leo later elaborated:

> I don't say that word because it disrespects women. I've learned that shit is messed up out here for women. We do this—men do this. So, I don't use that word, and I check people who use it. . . . We have to help women and make the world a better place for everyone. Abuse and sexism hurts everyone, not just the person who [is targeted]. . . . We have to be brave and make a change.

Students, through reflecting on their respective experiences individually and collectively, came to distinct realizations about their lived experiences and how those events affected others and themselves. Leo realized that his father's treatment of his mother resulted from sexism, patriarchy, and toxic masculinity, and not his father's "bad temper." Leo recognized individuals must actively counter the way men, and society, oppress women.

Overall, students named the injustices they had experienced and provided an analysis of the issues they identified, and began to see how classmates and themselves were affected by these issues. Further, the skill of reading and analyzing oppressive experiences from a larger systemic level was also demonstrated when students engaged with different texts via the mandated classroom curriculum.

APPLYING A CRITICAL SOCIOPOLITICAL ANALYSIS

"There's No Evidence to Support What Police Officers Do"

In the larger context of the Black Lives Matter movement garnering national attention, many students shared a distrust and fear of police officers during their Educational Journeys—the most prevalent theme students identified throughout all of their presentations. In response to the experiences of students, rather than teaching the mandated nonfiction unit focused on Carol Dweck's "growth mindset," the teacher created and taught a unit focused on police brutality. Although the teacher changed the unit content, they focused on the academic skills and CCSS of the original unit (i.e., introduce precise claims, cite strong and thorough textual evidence, and write objective summaries).

When the teacher introduced the unit, students completed an individual writing activity in response to the question: "'Black Lives Matter' or 'All Lives Matter'?" Students then engaged in a whole-class discussion to answer the question. After the discussion, students were given two texts to read: (1) a newspaper article that used statewide data to calculate how many people, based on race, were murdered by police officers the previous year, and (2) an interview of Richard Sherman, a Black football player who declared that "all lives matter." The next day, students had a whole-class discussion where they used the two texts to revisit the original question.

During the second discussion, students began to make nuanced arguments. For example, rather than focusing on the raw numbers where 43% of those killed by police officers were Latinx, 30% were White, and 20% were Black, students discussed the fact that Black people were disproportionately more likely to be killed by police officers—a rate almost five times higher than Latinx and White people. Letty posed a question to the class, asking, "How can someone look at these numbers and not think African Americans are targeted?" She answered her own question, stating, "It's racism against African Americans. These numbers don't just happen by themselves—it's no accident." Rather than taking the raw numbers at face value, and rather than asking what Black people are doing to be murdered at such high rates, Letty problematized the situation to see how systems played a role in police killings of Black people.

The students then shifted the discussion to focus on what, historically and contemporarily, has influenced how society, and by extension police officers, view and treat certain racial groups. Letty shared, "Whites tend to be viewed and treated in a more positive way [in society]" and that contemporary state-sanctioned violence against Black people was "an extension of slavery and Jim Crow [and] a long history of nobody caring about how African Americans are treated." Students began to articulate how the multiple forms of oppression Black people endure is by design, the intended consequence of various institutions.

"There's Nothing 'Good' About That Neighborhood"

The following curricular unit was focused on fictional texts. Students read *A Raisin in the Sun*, a play about the Youngers—a Black family—attempting to move into an all-White neighborhood in 1950s Chicago. The teacher integrated the topics of racial and linguistic segregation, other prominent themes students identified throughout their Educational Journeys. Building on the previous unit, the teacher focused on solidifying the same academic skills, adhering to similar standards as the previous unit.

When beginning the unit, students read, annotated, and discussed multiple informational texts (e.g., a Department of Housing and Urban Development report and national newspaper articles) to better understand historical and modern-day housing and school segregation in Chicago and in their own neighborhoods. This was accomplished by providing students with texts that explained racially restrictive covenants, redlining, and gentrification. This information allowed students to make a more informed and systematic reading and analysis of the time period of the play and the realities of the text's characters, and a more profound historical and contemporary understanding of their own communities.

In particular to *A Raisin in the Sun*, students were able to better understand and analyze the systemic factors that affected the Younger family at the internal and interpersonal levels. One example of this understanding and analysis was during a whole-class discussion, where students discussed the Younger family deciding to move into the all-White neighborhood. "Walter is already an angry alcoholic, he won't be able to deal with the racism in the new neighborhood" and "If the pain of racism made [Walter] abusive toward [his wife], it will only get worse in the new home" were two examples of ideas Letty posed to the class.

Students went beyond what can be perceived as a "happy ending" of the play. In fact, students critiqued this idea, lamenting what the family would endure attempting to live in a neighborhood where individuals did not want them, discussing the physical and emotional toll different forms of oppression would cause various family members at the internal, interpersonal, and institutional levels.

The centering prevalent themes students identified in their Educational Journeys created a classroom community and curriculum in which students could see their own lived experiences in different contexts. This learning environment helped students develop a better understanding of various forms of oppression beyond their own experiences, particularly as they analyzed "academic texts" as part of the mandated curriculum.

Prior to Educational Journeys, students would identify—based on their own lives and/or texts read in class—issues of racism, sexism, and other forms of oppression, but would not offer any analysis. Now, individually and collectively, students moved beyond simply naming social issues, and now analyzed how these issues affected themselves and others in profound ways.

The use of Educational Journeys as a pedagogical and curricular approach had tremendous personal and academic benefits for students—individually, collectively, and as a classroom community. This approach to teaching is an example of how to engage Latinx multilingual students, who are often provided with inadequate and bland learning environments, with pedagogy and curriculum that centers their lived experiences. In doing so, students foster a classroom community in which they are able to name and analyze various forms of oppression they and others endure in their daily lives. This community then allows students to simultaneously develop various academic competencies and a sociopolitical analysis.

REFERENCES

Annamma, S. (2016). Disrupting the carceral state through education journey mapping. *International Journal of Qualitative Studies in Education, 29*(9), 1210–1230.

Camangian, P. (2010). Starting with self: Teaching autoethnography to foster critical caring literacies. *Research in the Teaching of English, 45*(2), 179–204.

Dabach, B. D. (2014). "I am not a shelter!": Stigma and social boundaries in teachers' accounts of students' experience in separate "sheltered" English learner classrooms. *Journal of Education for Students Placed at Risk (JESPAR), 19*(2), 98–124.

Duncan-Andrade, J. M. R. (2009). Note to educators: Hope required when growing roses in concrete. *Harvard Educational Review, 79*, 181–194.

Garcia, A., & Dutro, E. (2018). Electing to heal: Trauma, healing, and politics in classrooms. *English Education, 50*(4), 375–383.

Genzuk, M. (2011). Specially designed academic instruction in English (SDAIE) for language minority students. *Center for Multilingual, Multicultural Research Digital Papers Series*. Center for Multilingual, Multicultural Research, University of Southern California.

Ginwright, S. (2010). *Black youth rising: Activism and radical healing in urban America*. Teachers College Press.

González, R. A. (2018). "Students with big dreams that just need a little push": Self-empowerment, activism, & institutional change through PAR *entremundos*. In J. Ayala, M. Cammarota, M. Berta-Ávila, M. Rivera, L. Rodríguez, & M. Torre (Eds.), *PAR EntreMundos: A Pedagogy of the Américas*. Peter Lang.

Gutiérrez, K. D., & Orellana, M. F. (2006). The "problem" of English learners: Constructing genres of difference. *Research in the Teaching of English, 40*(4), 502–507.

Howard, T. C. (2001). Telling their side of the story: African-American students' perceptions of culturally relevant teaching. *The Urban Review, 33*(2), 131–149.

Martínez, D. C., Rojo, J., & González, R. A. (2019). Speaking Spanish in White public spaces: Implications for literacy classrooms. *Journal of Adolescent & Adult Literacy, 62*(4), 451–454.

McFarland, J., Hussar, B., Wang, X., Zhang, J., Wang, K., Rathbun, A., Barmer, A., Forrest Cataldi, E., & Bullock Mann, F. (2018). *The condition of education 2018* (NCES 2018–144). National Center for Education Statistics.

Rodríguez, L. (2018). The educational journeys of students of color across the educational pipeline: A pedagogy of storytelling or a struggle for freedom? *Diaspora, Indigenous, and Minority Education, 12*(4), 214–229.

Tuck, E. (2009). Suspending damage: A letter to communities. *Harvard Educational Review, 79*(3), 409–428.

Umansky, L. M. (2018). According to plan? Examining the intended and unintended treatment effects of EL classification in early elementary and the transition to middle school. *Journal of Research on Educational Effectiveness, 11*(4), 588–621.

Valenzuela, A. (1999). *Subtractive schooling: U.S.-Mexican youth and the politics of caring*. State University of New York Press.

Warren, C. A. (2021). *About centering possibility in Black education*. Teachers College Press.

Chapter 8

Linking Multicultural Education With Best Practices for Multilingual Students

Renee Shank and Lin Wu

Over the past decades, multilingual students have gained increased access and learning opportunities, including comprehensible input, lowering the affective filter, and academic vocabulary development (Krashen, 1982). More recently, other practices have highlighted balanced opportunities for listening, speaking, reading, and writing (Echevarria et al., 2016); cultivating metalinguistic awareness by making connections across languages (Beeman & Urow, 2012); and deepening content knowledge through strategic primary language use (García et al., 2016). Although these research-based best practices provide multilingual students access to the English language, their home language and culture should be fully integrated during planning and instruction.

MULTICULTURAL EDUCATION

Multicultural education grew out of the U.S. Civil Rights movement during the 1960s and gradually evolved into a discipline aiming to reform schools and promote justice (Gay, 2020). Many scholars have contributed to expanding the knowledge of successful teaching practices for ethnically diverse students of color. These include but are not limited to educating Asian American and Pacific Islander students (Pang & Cheng, 1998), African American students (Ladson-Billings, 2009), Indigenous students (McCarty & Lee, 2014), and Latinx students (España & Herrera, 2020). In this chapter, the authors connect Banks's (2019) five dimensions of multicultural education with common lesson plan frameworks for teaching multilingual students and use case examples to illustrate how to translate these theories into practice in classrooms.

According to Banks (2019), the five dimensions of multicultural education are content integration, knowledge construction, prejudice reduction, equity pedagogy, and empowering school culture. *Content integration* requires teachers to logically infuse accurate ethnic, racial, and cultural content into school curricula, while *knowledge construction* encourages students to examine curricula through various frames of reference. Using various learning activities to build students' positive attitudes toward different groups anchors *prejudice reduction* while centering student voices and promoting communal academic achievement exemplifies *equity pedagogy*. When enacting these curricular and pedagogical techniques, teachers can create an *empowering school culture* that addresses social inequities and validates students from diverse backgrounds.

THEMATIC UNIT: KNOWLEDGE CONSTRUCTION

Thematic unit is instrumental in ensuring that multilingual students' linguistic needs are taken into account. Beeman and Urow (2012) argued that teachers must create cohesive thematic units with mandated district curricula when prioritizing language learning. At the same time, teachers should apply the principle of knowledge construction (Banks, 2019) to ensure that students have ample opportunities to learn about different cultures through various frames of reference. In linking these principles, teachers can help multilingual students enhance language learning, develop multiple viewpoints, cultivate critical thinking, and nurture cross-cultural empathy. Below, we provide an example of infusing knowledge construction with a thematic unit.

KNOWLEDGE CONSTRUCTION IN THEMATIC UNIT

Grade Level: 4th grade
Thematic Unit: Missions in California (Misiones en California; 加州的传教团)
Unit Objectives: Students will understand how Indigenous peoples in California (e.g., Ohlone, Pomo, Tongva) were affected by California's mission system by studying its history.
Language Objectives: These will be defined in individual lessons within the unit.

Unit Vocabulary in English: Self-determination, tribal sovereignty, sustainable farming, Camino real, missions, priests, disease, colonization

Unit Vocabulary in Spanish: autodeterminación, soberanía tribal, agricultura sostenible, camino real, misiones, sacerdotes, enfermedades, colonicacción

Unit Vocabulary in Mandarin Chinese: 自主，部落主权，可持续农耕，皇家公路，传教团，教士，疾病，殖民

Materials: California State History Elementary textbook. Zinn project curriculum on the mission system in California. *Life of the California Coast Nations* (Aloian & Kalman, 2004).

Description: Per California state standards, all fourth-grade students must learn about the mission system. Particularly, students must understand that the development of the mission system pushed Indigenous peoples to live on reservations and denied their right to self-determination. However, they sustained themselves and their communities by using some of the methods taught by the Catholic clergy.

Language Supports: Chunking texts into small pieces to ensure comprehension; drawing timelines; multiple opportunities to read and comprehend texts; sentence frames to support writing; using art to depict diverse perspectives; and using visuals to scaffold vocabulary.

PLANNING FOR INSTRUCTION: CONTENT INTEGRATION AND PREJUDICE REDUCTION

Echevarria et al. (2016) created a framework called the structured instruction and observation protocol (SIOP), which entailed teachers making language input comprehensible, clarifying what vocabulary will be used, and determining whether or not multilingual students will be assessed on their ability to listen, speak, read, or write. However, SIOP does not require cultural relevance for lesson content, which may hinder multilingual students' language production. Hence, content integration complements SIOP in developing multilingual students' language repertoires through the filter of their lived experiences (Banks, 2019).

Krashen (1982) argued that multilingual students have an affective filter that necessitates an environment conducive to learning a new language. When correcting multilingual students' speech errors, teachers should focus on the language objective to foster such an environment (Brandl, 2007). Through thoughtful revoicing and modeling, teachers can affirm multilingual students and encourage them to practice speaking. This approach aligns with prejudice reduction as teachers validate multilingual students' developing linguistic repertoires while helping them practice English (Banks, 2019). The following section provides a sample lesson on facilitating content integration and prejudice reduction in teaching and learning.

LESSON ON CONTENT INTEGRATION AND PREJUDICE REDUCTION

Grade Level: 2nd grade
Context of the Lesson: This lesson is a part of a thematic unit on the cultural significance of food. Students have been studying different types of food worldwide and sharing food vital to them and their families.
Language Objective: Students will learn to verbally state what they *ate* for dinner last night by practicing with their elbow partner.
Lesson Vocabulary in English: eat, dinner, last night
Lesson Vocabulary in Spanish: comer, cena, anoche
Lesson Vocabulary in Mandarin Chinese: 吃，晚饭，昨晚

Lesson Excerpt:

Teacher: Scholars, we have been learning about different types of food around the world over the past few days. Today, we will study the different food you eat at home. Can you all look at the board and repeat the language objective after me, "I will learn to verbally state what I *ate* for dinner last night."

Students: I will learn to verbally state what I ate for dinner last night.

Teacher: Great! For the next two minutes, I want you to turn and talk to your elbow partner about what you *ate* for dinner last night.

After two minutes . . .

Teacher: Scholars, let's come back as a group! I'm curious to learn about what you shared. We will start with Lily! Lily, what did you eat for dinner last night?

Lily: Last night, I eat pork, celery, and steam rice.

Teacher: I appreciate your efforts, Lily. Last night *I ATE, I ATE* pork, celery, and steamed rice. I know I asked what did you eat last night, but when you say it, you say *I ATE*. Thank you, Lily!

Teacher: Marco, what did you eat for dinner last night?

Marco: Last night, I eat chicken, noodles, and stream beans.

Teacher: I appreciate your efforts, Marco. Last night *I ATE, I ATE* noodles, chicken, and string beans. I know I asked what did you eat last night, but when you say it, you say *I ATE*. Thank you, Marco!

Lesson Debrief: The teacher started the lesson by referring to the different food students studied and introducing content relevant to students' lives. After getting students to repeat the language objective, the teacher instructed students to converse with each other on the lesson topic. Afterward, the teacher called on two multilingual students, Lily and Marco, to share with the class. Lily made an error in pronouncing steamed rice, and Marco pronouncing string beans. However, the teacher revoiced what both students said, corrected all errors, and only emphasized the one related to the language objective. In so doing, the teacher demonstrated successful practices of content integration and prejudice reduction.

LESSON IMPLEMENTATION: EQUITY PEDAGOGY

Many scholars suggest that translanguaging can improve multilingual students' acquisition of content. García et al. (2016) defined *translanguaging* as teachers' pedagogical and students' performative acts to move between languages fluidly and purposefully. It entices multilingual students to draw on their linguistic resources to process new academic content. Another benefit is that translanguaging validates multilingual students' ethnic identity and cultural heritage (Creese & Blackledge, 2015). This practice is equity pedagogy, as it centers on multilingual students' voices to promote academic achievement (Banks, 2019). Below, we provide a sample lesson of equity pedagogy in action.

Equity Pedagogy in Action

Grade Level: 5th grade

Lesson Objective: Students will explain how electricity moves through a circuit and travels from different sources to their homes by practicing and recording their observations.

Language Objective: Students will explain their observations in languages comfortable to them. Students will also use sentence stems to verbalize how electricity moves in English.

Lesson Vocabulary in English: lightbulb, battery, circuit, electricity, current

Lesson Vocabulary in Spanish: foco, batería, circuito, electricidad, corriente

Lesson Vocabulary in Mandarin Chinese: 灯泡，电池，电路，电，电流

Materials: Batteries, wires, lightbulbs, pen, paper, and bilingual visual representations of an electric circuit in Mandarin Chinese and Spanish.

Procedure: The teacher will demonstrate connecting wires to a battery to make a lightbulb light up. Students will then practice this on their own and document their observations. This documentation can be written in students' language choice or a mixture of languages.

Other scholars emphasized developing multilingual students' oracy. Beeman and Urow (2012) defined *oracy* as the oral production and reception of language. They observed that multilingual students are more likely to enhance their oracy when teachers use multilingual visual representations, strategic think-pair-share, flexible hand gestures, and total physical response during instruction. This approach is consistent with equity pedagogy, which includes "using a variety of teaching styles and approaches that are consistent with the wide range of learning styles within various cultural and ethnic groups" (Banks, 2019, p. 18). Below, we include a lesson in action incorporating translanguaging, oracy, and equity pedagogy.

TRANSLANGUAGING, ORACY, AND EQUITY PEDAGOGY IN ACTION

Grade Level: 3rd grade

Thematic Unit: Metamorphosis in frogs (metamorfosis en ranas; 青蛙的转变)

Unit Objective: Students will understand that tadpoles and frogs are the same species yet have different anatomy by studying metamorphosis.

Lesson Objective: Students will identify different parts of a frog's anatomy by practicing with their teachers and peers.

Language Objective: Students will verbalize different parts of a frog's anatomy in Mandarin Chinese, Spanish, or English by using translanguaging.

Lesson Vocabulary in English: frog, tadpole, anatomy, trunk, belly, legs, eyes, head, hind

Lesson Vocabulary in Spanish: rana, renacuajo, anatomía, tórax, barriga, piernas, ojos, cabeza, trasera

Lesson Vocabulary in Mandarin Chinese: 青蛙，蝌蚪，解剖，躯干，腹部，腿，眼睛，头，后腿

Materials: Large-scale drawing of a frog and a tadpole with labels of different body parts.

Lesson Procedure

Teacher: We have two pictures up here. Can one person tell me what this picture is in a language you feel comfortable using (pointing to the frog)?

Student 1: A frog.

Teacher: Great! And what about this one (pointing to the tadpole)?

Student 2: un pescado.

Teacher: Oh, you think it's a fish?

Student 3: 一条蜥蜴。

Teacher: Can someone tell me what this word is in English?

Student 4: A lizard.

Teacher: One of you said it's a fish, while the other said it's a lizard. Thank you for your effort! It is actually a tadpole, a baby frog. Can everyone say "tadpole"?

Students: Tadpole!

Teacher: Great! Now say "tadpole" to the person sitting next to you!

Students: Tadpole!

Teacher: Now say it to your elbow!

Students: Tadpole!

Teacher: Now say it to the floor!

Students: Tadpole!

Teacher: Wonderful! Today, we will talk about the difference between a tadpole (a baby frog) and a grown-up frog. We will start by examining different parts of their bodies. Look at these pictures of the tadpole and the frog. Turn and talk to your elbow partner for 30 seconds about the body parts you see in these pictures.

After 30 seconds . . .

Teacher: Alright, now I need volunteers to help us write the names of these body parts on the pictures. Can one of you tell me what you see in this picture of the frog in a language you feel comfortable using while pointing to your body part?

Student 5: I see eyes (pointing to eyes).

Teacher: Great (labeling the eyes)! What else do you see?

Student 6: I see— veo una cabeza (pointing to head).

Teacher: Awesome (labeling the head)! What else do you see?

Student 7: I see— 我看见了腿 (pointing to legs).

Teacher: Fabulous (labeling legs)! How many legs do you think it has?

Student 8: Four!

Teacher: Wonderful! The legs in the front are called front legs, and the legs in the back are called hind legs. Can you all say "hind" and gesture behind?

Students: Hind (while gesturing behind)!

Teacher: Turn to the back of the room and say "hind"!

Students: Hind (while turning to the back of the room)!

Teacher: Wonderful! What else do you see?

Student 9: I see the body.

Teacher: Alright, this is actually called the trunk. Can you all say "trunk" and do this (creating a gesture associated with the trunk that shows its shape)?

Students: Trunk (making the gesture)!

Teacher: Great! Can you turn to your partner and say "trunk" while making the gesture?

Students: Trunk!

Teacher: Where should I label the trunk?

Student 10: por atras (pointing to the back).

Teacher: Right! So, what about this part (pointing to the belly)?

Student 11: 是不是这里 (pointing to the stomach)?

Teacher: Yes! That is called the belly (labeling belly). Can you all say "belly" and rub yours?

Students: Belly (rubbing their bellies)!

Teacher: Wonderful! Now, when I count to three, turn and talk to your partner for 30 seconds about the different body parts you see in this picture of the tadpole.

Conclusion: The lesson concludes with students naming and comparing the parts of a tadpole's body and a frog's body.

CONCLUDING THOUGHTS

Although research on multicultural education and teaching multilingual students has been somewhat separate, there is a logical connection when addressing these students' learning needs. Linking these theories in thematic units, lesson planning, and instruction validates multilingual students' linguistic identity and cultural assets. It also creates an empowering school culture that promotes academic rigor and mutual respect. Regardless of their English proficiency, multilingual students can excel when practices such as those outlined in this chapter are adequately executed to maximize their performance.

REFERENCES

Aloian, M., & Kalman, B. (2004). *Life of the California coast nations.* Crabtree Publishing.

Banks, J. A. (2019). Multicultural education: Characteristics and goals. In J. A. Banks & C. A. M. Banks (Eds.), *Multicultural education: Issues and perspectives* (10th ed., pp. 3–24). Wiley.

Beeman, K., & Urow, C. (2012). *Teaching for biliteracy: Strengthening bridges between languages.* Caslon.

Brandl, K. (2007). *Communicative language teaching in action: Putting principles to work.* Pearson.

Creese, A., & Blackledge, A. (2015). Translanguaging and identity in educational settings. *Annual Review of Applied Linguistics, 35,* 20–35.

Echevarria, J., Vogt, M., & Short, D. (2016). *Making content comprehensible for English learners: The SIOP model* (5th ed.). Pearson.

España, C., & Herrera, L. Y. (2020). *En comunidad: Lessons for centering the voices and experiences of bilingual Latinx students.* Heinemann.

García, O., Ibarra Johnson, S., & Seltzer, K. (2016). *The translanguaging classroom: Leveraging student bilingualism for learning.* Caslon.

Gay, G. (2020). The reaffirmation of multicultural education. In H. P. Baptiste & J. H. Writer (Eds.), *Visioning multicultural education: Past, present, future* (pp. 9–24). Routledge.

Krashen, S. (1982). *Principles and practice in second language acquisition.* Pergamon Press.

Ladson-Billings, G. (2009). *The dreamkeepers: Successful teachers of African American children* (2nd ed.). Jossey-Bass.

McCarty, T. L., & Lee, T. S. (2014). Critical culturally sustaining/revitalizing pedagogy and indigenous education sovereignty. *Harvard Education Review, 84*(1), 101–124.

Pang, V. O., & Cheng, L. L. (Eds.). (1998). *Struggling to be heard: The unmet needs of Asian Pacific American children.* State University of New York Press.

Chapter 9

Beyond Language

A Sociocultural Approach to K–12 English Language Teaching and Learning

Immaculée Harushimana

> When those who have power to name and to socially construct reality choose not to see you or hear you, whether you are dark-skinned, old, disabled, female, or speak with a different accent or dialect than theirs, when someone with the authority of a teacher, say, describes the world and you are not in it, there is a moment of psychic disequilibrium, as if you looked into a mirror and saw nothing. Yet you know you exist and others like you, that this is a game with mirrors. It takes some strength of soul—and not just individual strength, but collective understanding—to resist this void, this nonbeing, into which you are thrust, and to stand up, demanding to be seen and heard.
>
> —Adrienne Rich

INTRODUCTION: TESOL GENESIS IN U.S. EDUCATION

The history of immigration in the United States challenges the very core principle of the Declaration of Independence, which was founded on the belief that "all men are created equal, that they are endowed by their Creator with certain unalienable Rights, that among these are Life, Liberty and the pursuit of Happiness." Historians' analyses (Massey, 2008) have revealed that immigrants from non-Western Europe did not receive the same welcome as their Western European counterparts. This observation is supported by the several lawsuits that were brought against different states by immigrant organizations and the Office of Civil Rights, who demanded educational justice.

Two famous cases include the 1974 *Aspira v. the Board of Education of New York City* court case, which led to the Consent Decree, which established bilingual instruction as a legally enforceable federal entitlement for New York City's non-English-speaking Puerto Rican and Latino students (Reyes, 2006). Another 1974 landmark case, *Lau v. Nichols*, lodged a complaint on behalf of numerous Chinese American students attending San Francisco public schools who felt that they were being denied educational opportunity because they did not speak English (Arias & Wiley, 2015; Sugarman & Widess, 1974).

Not long ago, the Office of Civil Rights filed a discrimination complaint for Somali refugees in Pittsburgh Schools for not giving them adequate services related to English as a second language instruction (Smydo, 2006). Similarly, the Minnesota chapter of the Council on American-Islamic Relations (CAIR) filed a harassment lawsuit against St. Cloud and Owatonna Schools on behalf of refugee children (Espinoza, 2010). In response to some of these cases, ESOL and bilingual education programs were established to address the noted injustices that were committed against immigrant children, most likely from non-Western backgrounds, by not giving them the support they needed in order to have a fair chance at academic success.

Ultimately, English Language Learning (ELL) pedagogy in K–12 school settings has placed high importance on the speedy acquisition of basic interpersonal communication skills (BICS) and cognitive academic language proficiency (CALP) skills (Cummins, 1979) meant to facilitate their academic integration and adaptation. The two major intervention approaches used to support English language learners—push in and pull out—suggest that academic integration was and remains the major mandate of ESOL programs.

Initially, this approach was aligned with the aspirations of immigrant parents, many of whom confessed that the main reason they immigrated was so that their children could have access to better education and a shot at a better life than they did. Unfortunately, unanticipated problems—including bullying, teachers' insensitivity to students' cultures, and cultural mismatches—made the dream unattainable for many parents (Harushimana, 2011, 2013; Raleigh & Kao, 2010). Social, cultural, and psychological dimensions need to be given serious consideration in English language teaching and learning.

PROBLEM AND PURPOSE

Research on underrepresented immigrant and refugee children has shown that addressing the language needs, without attending to the social and psychological integration needs of marginalized immigrant learners, does not guarantee academic success (Agyepong, 2013; Harushimana & Awokoya, 2011; Harushimana, 2011, 2013; Mthethwa-Sommers & Kisiara, 2015).

African immigrant and Middle Eastern children's narratives of schooling in the United States (Agyepong, 2013; Ahmad & Szpara, 2003; Harushimana, 2013; Traoré, 2006) have revealed that these children, especially those coming from underrepresented (and undesired) groups and cultures, have a very difficult time adjusting to the U.S. school environment and culture. TESOL programs need to ensure that ESOL teachers, the majority of whom are of Caucasian background, are culturally aware of the challenges incurred by these children both inside and outside the classroom.

This chapter draws from the emerging scholarship on the educational experiences of underrepresented immigrant children and youth to highlight the need for U.S. K–12 schools to (1) tailor the ESOL curriculum to the social lives and cultural realities of *all* children, (2) empower the students by giving them opportunities to appreciate and showcase the greatness of their home societies and cultures, (3) create a safe learning atmosphere for the students by showing willingness to learn the true facts about immigrant students' cultural histories, and (4) enrich the curriculum by incorporating newly learned facts about students' cultures in the curriculum. A special recognition will be paid to intellectual, scientific, historical, and literary achievements by some illustrious men and women from Africa, Asia, South Asia and Southeast Asia, and the Middle East to supplement Eurocentric materials.

THE RELEVANCE OF CULTURALLY RESPONSIVE PEDAGOGY IN TESOL

While the TESOL (Teaching English to Speakers of Other Languages) organization defines its mission as being to advance expertise in English language teaching, English Language Learners (ELLs) comprise primarily immigrant individuals who have immigrated with their own cultures, languages, and worldviews. Viewed from that lens, ELLs are de facto multicultural learners, but is TESOL pedagogy compatible with multicultural education?

Jim Cummins (1986), a prominent scholar in and advocate for bilingual education, has remarked that, sadly, schools are found to remain silent about issues of culture and identity and resistant to the idea of bringing diversity and equity to the schools (106–107). Because ESOL teachers are supposedly the main gate for non-English-speaking students into schooling, ideally, they should be acquainted with culturally responsive pedagogy. However, the TESOL curriculum reflects little multicultural content.

Multicultural education scholars rightly posit that (White) teachers of culturally diverse students cannot teach *what* they do not know (Howard, 2016); nor can they teach *who* they do not know. Due to the rapid expansion of globalization and the intensification of immigration, TESOL pedagogy needs to center culturally relevant teaching in its teacher-preparation curriculum, and English instruction for ELLs should incorporate the cultural practices and learning experiences that these children are bringing with them. Accordingly, ESOL teachers should be trained to use "the cultural knowledge, prior experiences, frames of reference, and performance styles of ethnically diverse students to make learning encounters more relevant to and effective for them" (Gay, 2013, p. 49–50).

It is important that teachers of ELLs understand the possible conflict that may occur between the way U.S.-born teachers understand diversity and how ELLs and their parents interpret it. From the U.S. classroom point of view, diversity differences oscillate "along dimensions of race, ethnicity, sexual orientation, gender, socioeconomic status, age, ability, religious or political beliefs, or other different ideologies" (Beveridge, 2020). Yet some of these distinctions may seem strange to immigrant students who may have a different understanding of diversity (i.e., linguistic, ethnic [tribal], regional, lineage structure, and marriage mores).

An educational system that does *not* pursue an assimilationist or subtractive agenda should make sure that mainstream U.S.-born teachers are educated about the different perceptions of diversity both from the U.S. point of view as well as from the foreign-born point of view. As Maxine Greene (1992) suggested, to live in an immigration country, like the United States, requires educators to be multiculturally mindful of an expanding community (i.e., one that keeps receiving new people with their own cultures that need to be respected).

MAKING CULTURE MATTER FOR ALL ENGLISH LANGUAGE LEARNERS

Soon after schools adhered to the Office of Civil Rights (OCR) mandate to accommodate the needs of non-English-speaking immigrant learners, it became clear that English language instruction was not the magic bullet that non-White immigrant students needed to succeed academically. In Ginley's

(1999) words, "majority" teachers need to understand that ELL students need more than just (White) teachers

> who tell the kids nicely to forget their Spanish and ask mommy and daddy to speak to them in English at home; who give them easier tasks so they won't feel badly when the work becomes difficult; who never learn about what life is like at home or what they eat or what music they like or what stories they have been told or what their history is. Instead, we smile and tell them to listen to our stories and dance to our music. We teach them to read with our words and wonder why it's so hard for them. We ask them to sit quietly and we'll tell them what's important and what they must know to "get ready for the next grade." And we never ask them who they are and where they want to go. (p. 86)

As Sonia Nieto (2011) rightly evoked, "The more distant a child's culture and language are from the culture and language of school, the more at risk that child is" (p. 321).

Through vigorous advocacy and activism, the Hispanic community in the United States has made significant strides in ensuring that the educational needs of Hispanic children are properly addressed. Bilingual education programs are majorly tailored to the needs of Hispanic children. Several educational resources are made available both in English and Spanish. Some ESL programs accommodate the needs of Hispanic children by assigning Hispanic teachers to teach ESOL kids, mainly because the majority of these children are of Hispanic descent (Agyepong, 2013).

Not only do these accommodations give the students a sense of pride in their culture, but also—most importantly—they facilitate the academic acquisition process. Unfortunately, this privilege has not been extended to immigrant children from other cultural and linguistic backgrounds, especially the new wave of immigrants from African nations and the Middle East. What about them? What happened to the content of the Declaration of Independence?

Greene (1992) has warned about the need for members of the classroom community to "remain aware of the distinctive members of the plurality who appear before each another with their own perspectives on the common, their own stories entering the culture's story, altering it as it moves through time" (1992, p. 259). It is true, as Greene believes, that in recent years "invisibility has been refused on many sides; [that] old silences have been shattered; [that] long-repressed voices are making themselves heard" (p. 250). The argument made in this chapter is that more work needs to be done in the example of leaders of immigrant and marginalized ethnic communities who have taken the bold initiative to create culturally minded (charter) schools.

CENTERING CULTURAL IDENTITY IN U.S. K–12 SCHOOLS: LESSONS FROM "NICHE CHARTER SCHOOLS"

Immigrant families' dissatisfaction with the K–12 educational system's disregard of their cultural practices has led some immigrant community activists to taking the situation into their own hands by creating either community language schools or ethnically themed charter schools that stress the importance of cultural maintenance among immigrant communities. The creation of these schools has created concerns among politicians (Eckes et al., 2011; Tintocalis, 2009), but that issue is beyond the scope of this chapter and will not be explored further.

Through their extensive research on bilingual community schools in New York, García and colleagues (2012) uncovered that bilingual education was the undertaking of different culturally minded institutions, such as churches, temples, synagogues, community-based organizations, storefronts, playgrounds, homes, hair-braiding salons, and many other places.

What brings these communities together, besides the recognition that they (or their forbears) originate from non-English-speaking societies and the commitment to maintaining their linguistic heritage "is that they are organized by parents and communities to ensure that their American children become bilingual and develop the multiple ethnolinguistic identities that will enable them to live in a global world" (García et al., 2012, p. xvii).

Niche schools—that is, ethnically or culturally oriented charter schools (Eckes et al., 2011)—may overlap with community language education in that they include heritage language learning in their curriculum; however, their main focus is on culture and religion. When community activist Sufyaan Mohammed was asked the rationale for pushing for the creation of a high school for Somali children in City Heights in San Diego, California, his response was, "Students when they come here they are acculturated or socialized in a different way that parents do not understand" (in Tintocalis, 2009, n.p.). In his welcome message, the principal, Dr. Elias Vargas, paraphrased the school mission as:

> to provide a rigorous and innovative college preparatory curriculum that is committed to working with our families and community members. School and home can work together to build skills and knowledge, to reinforce values and to develop a strong sense of self-confidence. We must invest our time and energies in our nation's most valuable resources—our children. (City Heights Preparatory High School, 2018)

School-home communication is a major challenge for immigrant families who come from culturally and linguistically underrepresented communities. There is likely to be a cultural and communication breakdown between teachers and parents. Examples of religious-conscious niche schools include Dugsi Academy in Minnesota and Almadinah School in New York City. What can TESOL programs do to address the concerns of the supporters of Dugsi Academy and Almadinah School philosophy?

TESOL AND THE INCLUSIVE MULTICULTURAL CURRICULUM

The creation of niche schools can be interpreted as immigrant parents' frustrated response to the mismatch between TESOL education and multicultural education goals. Whereas "multicultural curriculum strives to present more than one perspective of a cultural phenomenon or an historical event" and reject the "idea that students should be Americanized, in reality, assumed they should conform to a white, Eurocentric cultural model" ("Multicultural Education/Curriculum," n.d.), the English language learning curriculum remains assimilationist and Eurocentric at best, centering on the inculcation of Eurocentric values and the perpetuation of linguistic imperialism.

Some ESOL teacher-preparation leaders may claim that subjects like world history or world literature demonstrate schools' efforts to implement diversity in the curriculum, and that such courses cover a wide variety of authors such that every student will feel included. This assumption is far from the truth. According to David Damrosch (2003), world literature is commonly known in North America as an established canon of Western masterpieces such as the works by Ernest Hemingway, William Shakespeare, Virginia Woolf, and Edgar Allan Poe. And yet, just as there are internationally acclaimed writers from the western world and North America, so exist great writers from other parts of the world, like Africa (e.g., Ngugi wa Thiong'o, Ama Ata Aidoo, and Wole Soyinka), Asia (e.g., Amy Tan, Mo Yan, and Kazuo Ishiguro), South Asia (e.g., Amitav Ghosh) and Southeast Asia (e.g., Hanif Kureishi), and the Middle East (e.g., Salman Rushdie), whose works should be taught all over the world. These illustrious people give pride to men and women of the countries they belong to, including those who emigrated.

To break away from the colonial curriculum, ESOL teacher preparation should ensure that the candidates take literature courses in cultural designated studies programs—such as Black studies, Middle Eastern studies, Mexican studies, or Latin American studies—to acquaint themselves with non-Western literatures that might be representative of the diversity of the student populations they could be entrusted with in the profession.

Even though these literary works are written in English and may still be inaccessible to most students, their use in the ELL classroom presents several advantages. First, they use cultural references that the students can relate to, and the probability that some parents are familiar with those works is very high. Second, the students who come from the authors' backgrounds can feel inspired and empowered by the realization that someone like them has made such a great accomplishment. Third, focus on such works increases the opportunity for classroom participation. Finally, the teacher gains information that allows him or her to connect with the students better.

The other area that needs to be diversified is social studies. There have been persistent complaints that world history curricula focus on European history, while very little time and space are allocated to non-Western history, especially that pertaining to developing nations and the Middle East. As of late, because of rising nationalist movements in most European countries and the United States, Islamophobia has created a hostile learning climate for Muslim students, mainly due to the misportrayal of Muslim people and Islam in textbooks and the classroom (Revell, 2012). Additionally, because of the U.S. educational system's allegiance to a Eurocentric curriculum, African and Middle Eastern children are usually denied the opportunity to discover and appreciate world contributions by great men and women from their background.

Again, just as there are Nobel Prize winners from the western world and North America, so are there Nobel prize winners from other parts of the world, like Africa (e.g., Wangari Mathai; Nelson Mandela), Asia (Mo Yan; Shuji Nakamura), South Asia (e.g., Rabindranath Tagore; Sir Chandrasekhara Venkata Raman) and Southeast Asia (e.g., Muhammad Yunus; Mohammad A. Salam), and the Middle East (e.g., Ahmed Zewahil; Yasser Arafat). These people's achievements need to be included in school curricula across the world, just like Nobel prize winners from western countries are showcased in textbooks. It is also important to ensure that inclusion of world icons embraces all races, all faiths, and all genders.

Evidently, contemporary immigration trends, through the significant rise in African, Middle Eastern, and South Asian immigrant statistics, have drastically changed the face of the United States. Naturally, a change of this magnitude would imply the need to adjust the educational system to accommodate the needs of the new immigrant populations and facilitate their integration in the new world. Records of OCR and CAIR court cases, however, suggest otherwise, and that is wrong.

The U.S. educational system may identify students of immigrant and refugee background primarily as English language learners; however, these students and their families identify themselves in terms of their national origins, their ethnic group, their religion, their gender identity, etc. Any effort a teacher makes to include language learners' histories and cultural experiences in a lesson is likely to increase the students' feeling of self-worth and belonging and positively impact learning. Depriving an immigrant/refugee child of his or her history, literature, and culture can have adverse effects on a child's identity development and intellectual acquisition. Not only does focus on western epistemologies efface and substitute the non-western child's cultural heritage, but it also imposes on him/her a new world view and a new lens from which to view and construct the world. As an illustration, in her famous TED Talk, Nigerian writer Ngozi Chimamanda Adichie recounts that, as a result of being exposed to British and American books, the characters of her early stories were so far removed from her African reality,

> So I was an early reader, and what I read were British and American children's books. [. . .] I wrote exactly the kinds of stories I was reading: All my characters were white and blue-eyed, they played in the snow, they ate apples, and they talked a lot about the weather, how lovely it was that the sun had come out. [. . .] We didn't have snow, we ate mangoes, and we never talked about the weather, because there was no need to. . . . (Facinghistory.org, n. pg.)

That is the danger of a Eurocentric curriculum that the rising social justice advocacy in TESOL is seeking to counter. In particular, such a curriculum does not fare well with contemporary immigrants, the majority of whom fit the description of refugees, who yearn to see their human dignity restored. Sponsors of niche and home language maintenance schools are rising against the disregard of immigrants' cultural and religious identities by an assimilationist pedagogical agenda for immigrants of non-Western backgrounds. To bridge extremes between assimilationism and self-isolationism, TESOL pedagogy needs to implement ELL-friendly approaches, such as translanguaging, code-switching, culture questing, and the use of bilingual resources. Also, and most importantly, TESOL programs need to promote a pedagogy of identity empowerment through adoption of a curriculum that is culturally additive and intellectually unbiased. Like children being educated in their motherland, immigrant and refugee children deserve access to an education that validates their cultural and academic funds of knowledge.

REFERENCES

Agyepong, M. (2013). Seeking to be heard: An African-born, American-raised child's tale of struggle, invisibility, and invincibility. In *Reprocessing race, language and ability: African-born educators and students in transnational America* (pp. 155–168). Peter Lang.

Ahmad, I., & Szpara, M. Y. (2003). Muslim children in urban America: The New York city schools experience. *Journal of Muslim Minority Affairs, 23*(2), 295–301.

Arias, M. B., & Wiley, T. G. (2015). Forty years after Lau: The continuing assault on educational human rights in the United States and its implications for linguistic minorities. *Language Problems and Language Planning, 39*(3), 227–244.

Beveridge, B. (2020, July 21). *Creative an inclusive workplace.* https://www.linkedin.com/pulse/creating-inclusive-workplace-brett-beveridge

City Heights Preparatory High School. (2018, August). http://www.cityheightsprep.org/wp-content/uploads/2018/08/Intro-Welcome-Letter.jpg

Cummins, J. (1979). Cognitive/academic language proficiency, linguistic interdependence, the optimum age question and some other matters. *Working Papers on Bilingualism, No. 19.*

Cummins, J. (1986). Empowering minority students: A framework for intervention. *Harvard Educational Review, 56*(1), 18–37.

Damrosch, D. (2003). *What is world literature?* Princeton University Press.

Eckes, S. E., Fox, R. A., & Buchanan, N. K. (2011). Legal and policy issues regarding niche charter schools: Race, religion, culture, and the law. *Journal of School Choice, 5*(1), 85–110.

Espinoza, A. (2010, May 25). Federal agency will investigate alleged harassment against Somali students. *MPR News.* https://www.mprnews.org/story/2010/05/25/stcloudschool-investigation

Facing History & Ourselves. (n.d.). Reading 2: The Danger of a Single Story. https://www.facinghistory.org/holocaust-and-human-behavior/chapter-1/danger-single-story

García, O., Zakharia, Z., & Otcu, B. (Eds.). (2012). *Bilingual community education and multilingualism: Beyond heritage languages in a global city* (Vol. 89). Multilingual Matters.

Gay, G. (2013). Teaching to and through cultural diversity. *Curriculum Inquiry, 43*(1), 48–57.

Ginley, M. (1999). Being nice is not enough. In S. Nieto (Ed.), *The light in their eyes: Creating multicultural learning communities* (pp. 85–86). Teachers College Press.

Greene, M. (1992). The passions of pluralism: Multiculturalism and the expanding community. *The Journal of Negro Education, 61*(3), 250–261.

Harushimana, I. (2011). Mutilated dreams: African-born refugees in U.S. secondary schools. *Journal for Peace and Justice Studies, 21*(2), 23–41.

Harushimana, I. (2013). Foreign-born minorities and American schooling: The African-born adolescent's plea. In I. Harushimana, C. Ikpeze, & S. Mthethwa-Sommers (Eds.), *Reprocessing race, language and ability: African-born educators and students in transnational America.* Peter Lang.

Harushimana, I., & Awokoya, J. (2011). African-born immigrants in U.S. schools: An intercultural perspective on schooling and diversity. *Journal of Praxis in Multicultural Education, 6*(1).

Howard, G. R. (2016). *We can't teach what we don't know: White teachers, multiracial schools.* Teachers College Press.

Massey, D. S. (Ed.). (2008). *New faces in new places: The changing geography of American immigration.* Russell Sage Foundation.

Mthethwa-Sommers, S., & Kisiara, O. (2015). Listening to students from refugee backgrounds: Lessons for education professionals. *Penn GSE Perspectives on Urban Education, 12*(1), 1–9.

Multicultural education/curriculum. (n.d.). *Encyclopedia of Children's Health.* Retrieved January 10, 2022, from http://www.healthofchildren.com/M/Multicultural-Education-Curriculum.html

Nieto, S. (2011). *Language, culture, and teaching: Critical perspectives for a new century.* Taylor & Francis.

Raleigh, E., & Kao, G. (2010). Do immigrant minority parents have more consistent college aspirations for their children? *Social Science Quarterly, 91*(4), 1083–1102.

Revell, L. (2012). *Islam and education: The manipulation and misrepresentation of a religion.* Trentham Books.

Reyes, L. (2006). The Aspira consent decree: A thirtieth-anniversary retrospective of bilingual education in New York City. *Harvard Educational Review, 76*(3), 369–400.

Smydo, J. (2006, May 23). City schools settle complaint filed for Somali refugees. *Pittsburgh Post-Gazette.* https://www.post-gazette.com/local/city/2006/05/23/City-schools-settle-complaint-filed-for-Somali-refugees/stories/200605230189

Sugarman, S. D., & Widess, E. G. (1974). Equal protection for non-English-speaking school children: Lau v. Nichols. *Calif. L. Rev., 62,* 157.

Tintocalis, A. (2009, April. 22). Ethnic charter schools: Good or bad? *KPBS News.* https://www.kpbs.org/news/2009/apr/22/ethnic-charter-schools-good-or-bad

Traoré, R. (2006). Voices of African students in America: "We're not from the jungle." *Multicultural Perspectives, 8*(2), 29–34.

Chapter 10

Becoming "Talent Scouts"
Identifying Gifted Potential in English Learners

Holly D. Glaser and Erica C. Meadows

English Learners (ELs) remain underidentified and underserved in gifted education in the United States. ELs comprise approximately 11% of students in the nation's schools, yet they represent less than 3% of enrollment in gifted programs (U.S. Department of Education, 2016a, 2016b). While many factors contribute to ELs' underrepresentation, teachers, as their primary referral source, have the greatest potential to effect change. Unfortunately, teachers report receiving scant professional learning in meeting ELs' unique academic and linguistic needs (de Jong et al., 2013). Yet, when adequately prepared as "talent scouts," teachers can recognize gifted potential in ELs that might otherwise have been overlooked.

    The purpose of this chapter is to explore the bodies of specialized knowledge teachers need in order to serve as advocates for their gifted ELs. An overview of the key elements of linguistically responsive pedagogy, culturally sustaining pedagogy, and current research in gifted education will be discussed, along with how each of these bodies of specialized knowledge relates to the identification of gifted ELs. Finally, recommendations will be shared for how school and district leaders might design a collaborative approach to addressing inequities and enacting social change in the gifted identification process.

THREE AREAS OF SPECIALIZED KNOWLEDGE

For teachers to effectively "talent scout," they must employ three bodies of specialized knowledge: linguistically responsive pedagogy, culturally sustaining pedagogy, and current research in gifted education. Teachers should develop an understanding of the unique characteristics and needs of ELs, the relationship between language and culture, and the impact of language and culture on demonstration and interpretation of giftedness. Fundamental to this interpretation is the concurrent understanding that giftedness is an evolving, rather than static, set of behaviors that is highly dependent on the sociocultural context in which it develops.

Linguistically Responsive Pedagogy

Linguistically responsive pedagogy begins with the understanding of how multilingualism conveys certain cognitive advantages to ELs. Research comparing monolinguals to multilinguals demonstrates that multilinguals display greater strengths in divergent thinking, sociolinguistic awareness, and inhibitory control. Because ELs are constantly utilizing multiple language systems, their capacity to think flexibly and creatively is heightened. Teachers who understand the cognitive advantages of multilingualism will automatically begin with the mindset that learning a new language is a strength, rather than a deficit.

Approaching multilingualism as a strength in the classroom allows teachers to engage in instruction that promotes deeper understanding of content and higher-level thinking. Translanguaging, or the way multilinguals utilize all of their linguistic resources to process academic content in a new language, is especially helpful for teachers to understand. Translanguaging allows the student to select and utilize the language that best supports their thinking and communication. This is particularly important when abstract or critical and creative thinking is required. Thus, providing opportunities for ELs to utilize their home language may lead to more frequent demonstration of higher-level thinking.

One of the most commonly cited characteristics of giftedness in ELs is rapid language acquisition. However, in order for teachers to understand if ELs are acquiring language rapidly, they must first understand how language is acquired.

Basic Interpersonal Communication Skills (BICS) is context-embedded social language ELs typically acquire within the first 1–3 years. However, Cognitive Academic Language Proficiency (CALP), or context-reduced academic language, is what is required for students to speak and write proficiently at an academic level. CALP, which includes abstract and specialized language such as vocabulary or the "talk moves" used during academic discussions, can take 5–7 years for ELs to develop (Cummins, 1979). An understanding of the language acquisition process helps teachers explicitly plan for scaffolds and explicit instruction in the academic language needed to make abstract or complex concepts comprehensible.

Linguistically responsive pedagogy goes beyond grammar to address both language scaffolding and instruction at the word, sentence, and discourse levels. *Discourse* in the traditional sense might imply what is spoken; however, *discourse* may also refer to written language. Academic discourse is more formalized and must be explicitly taught for ELs to be able to demonstrate critical and creative thinking in English. Through explicit teaching of the academic discourse of talk and text used in the classroom, gifted ELs will be better equipped to demonstrate their full capabilities.

ELs can be engaged in cognitively demanding tasks as full and legitimate participants only if the instruction offered is both challenging and supported. Learning activities should be rigorous and connected to students' background knowledge. Teachers who have internalized these key concepts from linguistically responsive pedagogy are better equipped to provide the opportunities necessary to both encourage and recognize the development of giftedness in ELs.

Culturally Sustaining Pedagogy

Paris and Alim define *culturally sustaining pedagogy* as one that "seeks to perpetuate and foster—to sustain—linguistic, literate, and cultural pluralism as part of schooling for positive social transformation and revitalization" (quoted in Ferlazzo, 2017, para. 5). The link between language and cultural identity and its impact on the classroom experience is both complex and significant. Language learning is a socially situated process that is closely tied to identity formation.

Issues of identity shape all facets of language and literacy development; students access literacy practices through their unique cultural and linguistic identity. Providing opportunities for ELs to connect with literature representative of their cultures may engage them in demonstrating critical thinking in ways that cannot be facilitated by literature of the dominant culture.

Cultural and linguistic identity may also impact ELs' ability to access classroom instruction and resources. Toohey (1996) observed a relationship between identity and participation. Students who were viewed as outsiders by their peers did not gain full access to the social and material resources in the classroom. Additionally, student identity presented differently when interacting with peers in the home language.

One way to support students as valued members of the gifted classroom is through building on students' funds of knowledge, which Moll and colleagues (1992) described as those "historically accumulated and culturally developed bodies of knowledge and skills" (p. 133) essential to our daily functioning. This funds of knowledge perspective, in which students' cultural and cognitive resources are viewed as potential sources of educational capital, combats deficit paradigms by honoring the knowledge and experiences students bring to school by using them as resources for their learning.

Current Research in Gifted Education

While the sociocultural context in which giftedness emerges might be heavily influenced by teachers' use of culturally sustaining pedagogy, another element crucial to defining how giftedness is socioculturally endorsed is the teacher's conception of giftedness. Teachers who hold outdated beliefs about what giftedness is and how it is displayed may fail to identify potential in students despite their use of culturally sustaining pedagogy.

Historically, giftedness has been viewed through entity-based theoretical models. These models promoted the idea that students either possess gifts/abilities/talents or they don't, and it was possible to measure such traits through psychometric assessments. Evolving conceptions of giftedness view giftedness as potential that develops over time and under certain circumstances. Teachers who define giftedness as a trait that is either possessed or not, or who perceive evidence of giftedness as high scores on assessments without attending to the work students produce in class, may inadvertently sabotage their own efforts to identify gifted potential in ELs.

In addition to understanding how conceptions of giftedness have evolved, teachers of gifted ELs should also recognize the larger historical and pervasive issue of underrepresentation in gifted education. Black, Hispanic, and Native American students, English Learners, students with disabilities, and students living in poverty are and continue to be underrepresented in gifted programs nationwide.

Intersectional data analyzed by Siegle (2016) has demonstrated that students from multiple underrepresented backgrounds (e.g., an English Learner who is Hispanic and living in poverty) have a much lower probability of being identified than their peers from non-underrepresented backgrounds (e.g., an English-proficient White student not living in poverty). These data have suggested that underrepresentation is exacerbated when viewed through an intersectional lens, and that identification processes must be viewed critically by teachers hoping to serve as "talent scouts" for gifted ELs.

IMPACT OF SPECIALIZED KNOWLEDGE ON THE GIFTED IDENTIFICATION PROCESS

While the gifted identification process varies across school districts, the most common components of the process include referral, assessment, rating scales, and collection of student work. Teacher knowledge of linguistically responsive pedagogy, culturally sustaining pedagogy, and current research in gifted education impacts each of these components.

Referral Process

Nominations, or referrals, are often the first stage in the identification process and, as such, are critically important. The way referrals are accepted varies. While parents or students may have the power to initiate the process, teachers are the most likely to make the referral, putting them in the position of gatekeeper and evaluator. This can be problematic if teachers have little or no knowledge of language development and the characteristics of giftedness in ELs.

In order to identify exhibitions of giftedness, teachers must understand how language proficiency and cultural differences impact student social interactions, behavior, and academic performance. They must also understand that a student's language skills can be developed concurrently within a gifted classroom given appropriate linguistic scaffolding.

Assessment

Ability assessments remain integral components of the gifted identification process, and their interpretation influences identification decisions. In order to appropriately contextualize these assessments, teachers should understand that results are not definitive indicators of giftedness, nor do scores remain static over time. They must base their interpretation of results on factors such as where students are along the second language acquisition continuum, how long they have attended U.S. schools, and the cultural and linguistic bias inherent in ability tests.

Considering that it takes 3–7 years for students to develop different aspects of language, there is a distinct possibility that ELs' scores on an ability test may change when retested. However, some school districts may only test students upon referral, instead of utilizing universal screening. Even in school districts where universal screening is implemented, ELs may only have one opportunity to take a test, possibly not even in their home language. These one-time scores may lead teachers to develop erroneous beliefs about gifted ELs' abilities.

Rating Scales

Many districts use rating scales in addition to assessments to allow teachers or families to provide additional information about a student during the identification process. Scales or checklists may or may not be research-based and can be used in a variety of ways, either as supplemental or required information. Additionally, teachers completing the scales may be unfamiliar with the characteristics considered typical of gifted ELs. Observing students in small-group ESOL instruction and other areas of strength may provide better opportunities for teachers to observe the gifted potential ELs may exhibit in different environments.

Student Work Samples

The collection of student work for the screening file is arguably that which is most impacted by the teacher, as it directly reflects the learning opportunities offered to students in the classroom. Teachers who understand how to design rigorous tasks that have been appropriately scaffolded for the language needs of ELs will likely provide samples that best reflect the academic capabilities of their students. However, if language is viewed as a deficit, or if students are not seen as legitimate participants, they may not receive opportunities to engage in critical and creative thinking—thereby limiting them to demonstrating only a remedial level of potential.

A COLLABORATIVE APPROACH TO ENACTING SOCIAL CHANGE IN GIFTED EDUCATION

Examining identification practices in the context of current inequities in gifted education is one method through which social change for ELs can be enacted. When ELs are not identified for gifted programs at the same rates as other student populations, districts must examine why and how this occurs, and do so through the lens of multiple stakeholders. A four-step process is suggested in designing this collaborative approach to improving identification outcomes for gifted ELs:

- Step 1: Identify a team of collaborators. Stakeholders within the school district should be selected who carry a range of expertise, including knowledge of gifted education, second language acquisition, curriculum

and instruction, and assessment. Families and community members, such as university personnel, may also be considered to lend outside perspective and experiences. Adopting a framework for improvement such as Improvement Science, Knowledge-to-Action Cycle, or Self-Study may help facilitate change.
- Step 2: Uncover the existing inequities in the local gifted program. Each local context is unique and, as such, should be examined in terms of not only underrepresentation of ELs but also underrepresentation of additional student populations. A thorough examination of the complexities of underrepresentation, including the impact of intersectionality on student identification, will lead to more refined targets for professional learning.
- Step 3: Examine current instructional and identification practices with an eye toward equity and inclusion. Given the inequities within the local context, work with the team of collaborators to take a critical look at how current instructional and identification practices might be contributing to the issue of representation in the local gifted program. Be prepared for some difficult discussions; after all, if the current practices were working, there would be no issues of underrepresentation in the local program. Challenge one another to be creative and to examine current research on best practice.
- Step 4: Design professional learning to support instruction and identification of gifted ELs. Professional learning should be tailored to educators' needs and based on what was uncovered in the collaborative group's work. Topics might include recognizing giftedness in ELs, designing rigorous yet accessible instruction for ELs, and understanding and advocating for ELs in the gifted identification process.

The pervasive issue of ELs' underrepresentation in gifted programs can be addressed through targeted professional learning, along with intentional decision-making by knowledgeable administrators and instructional leaders. The key ingredient, however, is an understanding of these three bodies of specialized knowledge and how they impact gifted identification processes.

This chapter briefly explored the knowledge, skills, and dispositions teachers need to become effective "talent scouts." Common features of the gifted identification process were examined through the lens of linguistically responsive pedagogy, culturally sustaining pedagogy, and current research in gifted education. Recommendations were offered for designing a collaborative approach to addressing inequities in gifted education. Teachers and school leaders equipped with this knowledge will be empowered to enact social change that provides the access to gifted services that ELs both need and deserve.

REFERENCES

Cummins, J. (1979). Cognitive/academic language proficiency, linguistic interdependence, the optimum age question and some other matters. *Working Papers on Bilingualism, 19.*

de Jong, E. J., Harper, C. A., & Coady, M. R. (2013). Enhanced knowledge and skills for elementary mainstream teachers of English language learners. *Theory Into Practice, 52*(2), 89–97.

Ferlazzo, L. (2017). Author interview: Culturally sustaining pedagogies. *EdWeek.* https://www.edweek.org/teaching-learning/opinion-author-interview-culturally-sustaining-pedagogies/2017/07

Moll, L. C., Amanti, C., Neff, D., & Gonzalez, N. (1992). Funds of knowledge for teaching: Using a qualitative approach to connect homes and classrooms. *Theory Into Practice, 31*(2), 132–141.

Siegle, D. (2016). *Research update from the NCRGE.* The National Center for Research on Gifted Education (NCRGE). http://ncrge.uconn.edu

Toohey, K. (1996). Learning English as a second language in kindergarten: A community of practice perspective. *Canadian Modern Language Review, 52*(4), 549–576.

U.S. Department of Education, Office for Civil Rights, Civil Rights Data Collection. (2016a). *Number and percentage of public school students enrolled in gifted/talented programs, by race/ethnicity, disability status, and English proficiency, by state: School year 2015–16.* Retrieved from http://ocrdata.ed.gov

U.S. Department of Education, Office for Civil Rights, Civil Rights Data Collection. (2016b). *Public school students overall and by race/ethnicity, students with disabilities served under IDEA and those served solely under Section 504, and students who are English language learners, by state: School year 2015–16.* Retrieved from http://ocrdata.ed.gov

Chapter 11

Introducing Translanguaging as Pedagogy

Unpacking Preservice ESL Teachers' Language Ideologies and Practices

Nuo Xu and Verónica E. Valdez

Language teaching and learning are not ideologically neutral practices. Curdt-Christiansen and Weninger (2015) define *ideology* not just as a system of beliefs, instead viewing it as "the dominant political, educational, or cultural value system that secures its legitimacy through institutionally circulated discourses, and through the impact of these discourses on readers/viewers/listeners" (p. 3). Teachers' language ideologies significantly impact their teaching attitudes and practices toward students' home languages and cultures (Iversen, 2019). It is thus important for teachers to reflect on the ways their individual language ideologies influence classroom practices and potentially create barriers to student learning with respect to plurilingual language development.

Many teacher-education programs prepare preservice teachers to be culturally and linguistically responsive educators (Skepple, 2015). Being culturally responsive means taking a critical stance on multicultural education (Nieto, 2017). With the increasing diversity of student populations in K–12 classrooms, it is essential to prepare prospective teachers with relevant knowledge and skills, particularly since teachers' backgrounds and perspectives often reflect more privileged middle-class, White values than those of many of their students (Skepple, 2015).

The majority of teacher candidates know little about culturally diverse groups and have not critically examined their beliefs about student differences

(Skepple, 2015). Therefore, it is essential to critically examine ways to articulate, deconstruct, and reimagine social-justice-oriented teacher education and activism. Combining culturally sustaining pedagogy (CSP; Paris, 2012; Paris & Alim, 2014) and translanguaging pedagogy (García & Leiva, 2014) offers an opportunity for this reimagination of multicultural, multilingual efforts in teacher education.

CULTURALLY SUSTAINING AND TRANSLANGUAGING PEDAGOGIES

CSP builds on Ladson-Billings's (1992) culturally relevant pedagogy (CRP). It helps analyze how instructional practices could be applied to tap into communicative and cognitive processes that address issues tied to equity, power, social justice, and democracy in teaching (Howard & Rodriguez-Minkoff, 2017).

Paris (2012) questioned whether the term *CRP* went far enough in helping youth of color maintain their linguistic and cultural ways of being while also helping them understand dominant practices. He proposed using the term *culturally sustaining pedagogy* instead (Paris & Alim, 2014, p. 88), advocating for the support of multilingualism and multiculturalism in practice as a means of sustaining the richness of our pluralist society.

For Paris (2012), what is sustained is inclusive of "all of the languages, literacies, and cultural ways of being that our students and communities embody-both those marginalized and dominant" (p. 96). CSP envisions a world where we decenter whiteness and contest iterations of White supremacist ideologies and practices (Paris & Alim, 2014). It provides opportunities for minoritized students to thrive by valuing their culture, language, and learning potential. We, like Ladson-Billings (2014), view CSP as an extension of CRP's original goals.

We also utilize García and Leiva's (2014) theory on translanguaging. This theory views students' use of their full linguistic repertoire and cultural identities as a mechanism for realizing the possibilities of social justice through the disruption of monoglossic ideologies.

In the United States, the monoglossic ideology of bilingualism, which essentially believes that one language plus another equals two languages (García & Leiva, 2014), is widely accepted across traditional teacher-preparation programs. This is problematic because it institutionalizes the dominance of English and the strict language-separation policies and practices that hinder the educational progress of students designated as English learners.

To challenge linguistic purism and hierarchies, translanguaging and translanguaging pedagogy have emerged as a new culturally sustaining approach for teachers (Kleyn & García, 2019). Translanguaging pedagogy emphasizes the dynamic use of multiple languages to enhance learning and make schools a more welcoming environment for multilingual children, families, and communities (MacSwan & Faltis, 2020). Central to translanguaging pedagogy is its transformational intent: transforming subjectivities and social structures (García & Leiva, 2014). Translanguaging contributes to new understandings of language ideology, pedagogy, and educators' views on multilingual students and their own language use in classroom settings.

This chapter aims to address how receiving instruction about translanguaging and translanguaging pedagogy through a teacher-education program influenced preservice teachers. Specifically examined are its influence on the language ideologies toward non-English languages and the enactment of culturally and linguistically sustaining practices toward students designated as English learners.

RESEARCH METHODOLOGY

This qualitative study draws on an archival research method (Ventresca & Mohr, 2017). Anonymized archival data was analyzed from one spring 2020 ESL methods course supervised by Author 2 and taught as part of a predominantly White public university's teacher-education program in the U.S. intermountain west.

The dataset included four teacher reflection notes (Author 1), as well as course assignments submitted by 24 preservice teachers prior to the introduction of translanguaging (10 week-4 group SIOP lesson plans) and after the introduction of translanguaging (10 group translanguaging lesson plans [García et al., 2017], eight group translanguaging visual artifacts, 48 individual week-6 and week-9 reading notes, and 18 week-13 individual discussion board posts on designing a culturally sustaining activity after the introduction of translanguaging).

A priori and open coding (Saldaña, 2021) initiated the thematic data-analysis process (Nowell et al., 2017). A priori codes included language ideologies toward English and non-English languages, language beliefs about bilingualism, approaches to bilingual education, culturally and linguistically responsive instructions and designed activities, and so on.

Some examples of emergent subcodes under language ideologies included monolingual ideologies, standard language ideologies, and translanguaging ideologies. Following the coding process, patterns emerged that led to the following themed findings across the data points: shifts toward translanguaging ideologies; teachers' pedagogical approaches moved toward more critical stances; and challenges to enacting translanguaging pedagogy.

FINDINGS

Findings revealed that preservice teachers shifted from theory learning to an actionable understanding of how K–12 schools could use translanguaging across grades and content areas. They engaged in critical conversations, worked collaboratively, planned culturally and linguistically sustaining practices using translanguaging approaches, and pinpointed challenges to their pedagogical implementation.

Shifts Toward Translanguaging Ideologies

Receiving instruction about translanguaging pedagogy shifted preservice teachers' language ideologies. Before the translanguaging class, 90% of the preservice teachers' group SIOP lesson plans reflected their English monolingual ideology that values English above non-English languages and traditional ways of understanding language and bi-/multilingualism. Although one group used culturally relevant examples in their SIOP lesson plans, most preservice teachers' strategies (e.g., small-group discussions, hands-on activities) adhered to using only English as the medium of instruction as a means to achieve a certain level of English-language proficiency without regard for students' multilingualism.

One group, for instance, described a student learning objective as "to understand common idioms in the English language," followed by teaching strategies of "using students' background knowledge to share their own idioms" and "working in small groups." Both were to be enacted only in English, followed by a review/assessment process of "sharing idioms with the class" in English only. Preservice teachers' emphasis on English at the exclusion of students' other languages mirrored what they had learned in their teacher-education program up to that point.

On the other hand, the course introduction of translanguaging and translanguaging pedagogy helped preservice teachers foster critical thinking about named national languages and related ideologies within power relations that systemically create linguistic hierarchies and categorizations within schools. Specifically, their translanguaging lesson plans, discussion board posts, and reading notes illustrated their transition to embracing a translanguaging ideology and the ways they took up a translanguaging stance (Kleyn & García, 2019).

After the introduction of translanguaging, 90% of the submitted group translanguaging lesson plans validated multilingualism and emphasized the need to bring in students' home languages. For example, two preservice teachers designed a lesson plan that had their students generate an artist statement and discuss their artwork using the language of art using all languages in students' linguistic repertoire, including multimodal elements. This suggests a shift in practice.

An ideological shift toward fostering critical thinking about English monolingualism, named languages, multilingual students, and multicultural education was also evident in all preservice teachers' individual reading notes. This was illustrated when a preservice teacher stated, "The translanguaging concept is a critical pedagogy that challenges the oppressive notion that there is a 'right' and 'wrong' language, and it preserves culture and educates all students through a lens of acceptance and respect."

Finally, 18 preservice teachers completed discussion board posts prompted by an end-of-semester request to design a "short [multicultural] activity based on the pedagogies . . . learned from the readings." Nine of these preservice teachers planned culturally sustaining activities based on an understanding of translanguaging as a tool for disrupting the linguistic hierarchy and liberation of silenced and marginalized voices. These nine preservice teachers were able to link translanguaging pedagogy to culturally sustaining practices despite the absence of a direct mention of translanguaging. They embraced students' home language practices in the classroom to promote language collaboration and the knowledge development of all students.

Teachers' Pedagogical Approaches Moved Toward More Critical Stances

Introducing translanguaging as pedagogy also facilitated preservice teachers' willingness to take on a critical stance. Preservice teachers' SIOP lesson plans prior to the introduction of translanguaging reflected a decidedly conservative or liberal stance (Jenks et al., 2001) toward implementing CSP. For example, one group described meeting their science language and content objectives using only English and ignoring the complex issues of cultural inclusionary practices.

Another group claimed to build students' background knowledge on the theme of "understanding oneself and appreciation of others," but students were to share everything using only English. Neither of these stances includes an examination of how the standardization around content excluded the voices and experiences of those not in power.

While teachers with a liberal view might appreciate diversity through a "colorblind" lens that discounts racial differences, teachers with a critical view understand and examine how racial inequities are reproduced in schooling. They also advocate for social justice as well as engage students in transformative ways (Dover et al., 2018). The preservice teachers' translanguaging lesson plans and discussion board posts reflected shifts in their pedagogical approaches toward a more critical and translanguaging stance (García et al., 2017).

For example, all translanguaging lesson plans included activities that connected to the cultures, languages, and knowledges of linguistically minoritized students' families and communities. They created room for students to demonstrate content knowledge using general linguistic and language-specific performances. Similarly, discussion board posts also illustrated a shift toward more critical stances. In particular, 4 out of 18 discussion board posts mentioned engaging students in conversations related to the sociopolitical context of education.

Preservice teachers allowed opportunities for students to discuss cultural diversity, identities, and their cultural histories rather than conform to the norms of Whiteness embedded in society, including schooling. For example, an activity was described in a discussion post that asked students to draw from their community resources, gather textiles that were meaningful to them, and sew the textiles together to create a collaborative, cohesive fabric workpiece. In another example, one French-English dual-immersion teacher designed a cultural/historical lesson based on the French/Algerian conflict by using a book that addressed many of the same issues immigrants in the United States face, such as inequality and language barriers.

Challenges to Enacting Translanguaging Pedagogy

Preservice teachers expressed concerns for the implementation of translanguaging pedagogies and the establishment of translanguaging spaces in schools and institutions in view of sometimes-conflicting perspectives. For example, reading notes indicated how monolingual pedagogical approaches and English-only curriculums often met parents' expectations for their children designated as English learners to develop the language proficiency necessary to pass standardized tests.

Also, some preservice teachers expressed a need for more diversified ways to ensure their lesson plans, units, and assessments would meet the translanguaging needs of students who had difficulty verbally communicating because they spoke no English or who spoke a number of languages not spoken by them. Such expressions of challenges shared through discussion posts and reading notes were helpful in examining how translanguaging in different contexts could be implemented and how to collaboratively bridge the gap between theory and practice in multilingual classrooms.

Findings demonstrate how the introduction of translanguaging pedagogy helped to unpack preservice ESL teachers' language ideologies and pedagogical practices. Preservice teachers shifted toward translanguaging ideologies, and their pedagogical approaches moved toward more critical stances focused on transforming subjectivities and social structures.

They encouraged students to bring their home language practices into classrooms to foster a deeper understanding of their current lived experiences. In designing translanguaging lesson plans, preservice teachers also encountered challenges in implementing translanguaging pedagogy that ranged from facing monolingual English-only policies and ideologies to struggles with managing the array of languages of their students.

This study introduces translanguaging pedagogy as an enactment of culturally sustaining pedagogy in a teacher-education program. Translanguaging pedagogy is particularly suited for working with multilingual and multicultural learners as it builds on the languages and cultural practices of students and positions both teachers and students as learners. It offers ways instructional spaces can be created to go beyond our traditional understanding of programs for multilingual learners and transform them.

As teacher educators, taking a translanguaging stance asks us and the preservice teachers we train to examine, confront, and unpack our beliefs and perspectives of education for multilingual students designated as English learners. It is equally important for teacher educators to provide preservice teachers with ample opportunities to take creative risks while designing meaningfully equitable instructional practices, such as adopting translanguaging pedagogy and other culturally sustaining practices. It is these opportunities that can create social change by transforming the educational experiences of multilingual students designated as English learners.

REFERENCES

Curdt-Christiansen, X. L., & Weninger, C. (2015). Introduction: Ideology and the politics of language textbooks. In X. L. Curdt-Christiansen & C. Weninger (Eds.), *Language, ideology and education: The politics of textbooks in language education* (pp. 1–8). Routledge.

Dover, A. G., Henning, N., Agarwal-Rangnath, R., & Dotson, E. K. (2018). It's heart work: Critical case studies, critical professional development, and fostering hope among social justice–oriented teacher educators. *Multicultural Perspectives, 20*(4), 229–239.

García, O., Johnson, S. I., & Seltzer, K. (2017). *The translanguaging classroom: Leveraging student bilingualism for learning.* Caslon.

García, O., & Leiva, C. (2014). Theorizing and enacting translanguaging for social justice. In A. Creese & A. Blackledge (Eds.), *Heteroglossia as practice and pedagogy* (pp. 199–216). Springer.

Howard, T. C., & Rodriguez-Minkoff, A. C. (2017). Culturally relevant pedagogy 20 years later: Progress or pontificating? What have we learned, and where do we go? *Teachers College Record, 119*(1), 1–32.

Iversen, J. Y. (2019). Negotiating language ideologies: Preservice teachers' perspectives on multilingual practices in mainstream education. *International Journal of Multilingualism*, 1–14.

Jenks, C., Lee, J. O., & Kanpol, B. (2001). Approaches to multicultural education in preservice teacher education: Philosophical frameworks and models for teaching. *The Urban Review, 33*(2), 87–105.

Kleyn, T., & García, O. (2019). Translanguaging as an act of transformation: Restructuring teaching and learning for emergent bilingual students. In L. C. de Oliveira (Ed.), *The handbook of TESOL in K–12* (pp. 69–82). Wiley.

Ladson-Billings, G. (1992). Liberatory consequences of literacy: A case of culturally relevant instruction for African American students. *The Journal of Negro Education, 61*(3), 378–391.

Ladson-Billings, G. (2014). Culturally relevant pedagogy 2.0: A.k.a. the remix. *Harvard Educational Review, 84*(1), 74–84.

MacSwan, J., & Faltis, C. J. (Eds.) (2020). *Codeswitching in the classroom: Critical perspectives on teaching, learning, policy, and ideology.* Routledge.

Nieto, S. (2017). Re-imagining multicultural education: New visions, new possibilities. *Multicultural Education Review, 9*(1), 1–10.

Nowell, L. S., Norris, J. M., White, D. E., & Moules, N. J. (2017). Thematic analysis: Striving to meet the trustworthiness criteria. *International Journal of Qualitative Methods, 16*(1), 1–13.

Paris, D. (2012). Culturally sustaining pedagogy: A needed change in stance, terminology, and practice. *Educational Researcher, 41*(3), 93–97.

Paris, D., & Alim, H. S. (2014). What are we seeking to sustain through culturally sustaining pedagogy? A loving critique forward. *Harvard Educational Review, 84*(1), 85–100.

Saldaña, J. (2021). *The coding manual for qualitative researchers.* SAGE.

Skepple, R. G. (2015). Preparing culturally responsive preservice teachers for culturally diverse classrooms. *Kentucky Journal of Excellence in College Teaching and Learning, 12*(6), 57–69.

Ventresca, M. J., & Mohr, J. W. (2017). Archival research methods. In J. A. C. Baum (Ed.), *The Blackwell companion to organizations* (pp. 805–828). Blackwell.

Chapter 12

Characteristics of English Language Learners

Nan Li and Courtney A. Howard

The fastest-growing segment of the American P–12 school population is English Language Learners (ELLs). In recent years, this group has increased at a remarkable pace in our school system. The National Center for Education Statistics (NCES, 2020) revealed that the ELL school population has reached 5.3 million with an increase rate of 29.7% over the past 10 years. The NCES (2020) data also showed that the growth of general school enrollment in the United States was only 5.7% during the same period. The ELL school population comprises about 20% of the total U.S. school enrollment, with some states having an even higher percentage (e.g., Texas, New Mexico, Nevada, and California).

The National Clearinghouse for English Language Acquisition (NCELA) also revealed that the number of ELL students enrolled in American public schools has increased by 51%, the highest increase in the last three decades (NCELA, 2020). The rapid increase in the ELL school population poses a unique challenge for the P–12 teachers in classrooms as they strive to ensure that their language-minority students will get the access to the core curriculum and acquire academic content knowledge while simultaneously they are also learning the English-language skills. It helps teachers to better work with ELLs when they understand the characteristics of the ELLs, especially related to their unique life and culture.

LIFE- AND CULTURE-RELATED CHARACTERISTICS

In 1968, the U.S. Congress voted to eliminate the Johnson-Reed Act, an immigration law created in 1924 with a quota system to discriminate against non-European immigrants (Li, 2015). Since then, the immigrant population in the United States has increased with a noticeable change in country sources (i.e., the immigration population represents more diversity in country origins). The national demographics affect school population.

The students whose primary language is not English have thus increased, especially from non-European countries. For example, ELL school enrollment increased by 105% from 1995 to 2005, with over 70% of ELLs being Hispanic students, but the general school population growth was less than 10% during the same period. With the new demographics in schools, effectively educating this unique school population has challenged the P–12 teachers in classrooms.

So who are ELLs, and what are some of their characteristics? Typically, an English Language Learner is defined as one whose first language (L1) is not English, who is in the process of learning English as a second language (L2), or who is not yet able to profit fully from English-only instruction and needs instructional support to fully access academic content (Li, 2015; NCELA, 2020). As the fastest-growing segment of the school population, the ELLs also represent a heterogeneous group of students with different life and cultural experiences.

They not only have diverse gifts, educational needs, and goals but also have different family backgrounds and languages. For example, some ELLs may live in their own cultural enclaves, while others may live in a non-ELL family community; some ELL families may live in the United States for over a generation, while other ELLs are newcomers; and some ELLs may be high achievers in schools, while other ELLs can be struggling readers. Thus, no single profile can represent the needs of all ELLs, nor can they be defined adequately with a single definition. Yet ELLs do have some characteristics that teachers need to know to better work with them and accommodate their learning needs.

The following are some contributing factors to the differences among ELLs. Each of these can affect ELLs' acquisition of English language skills and content knowledge as they are entering American schools:

- length of residence in the United States;
- literacy skills in the primary language(s) and previous schooling;
- education of parents, socioeconomic status, and resources available at home; and

- personal life experiences and cultural norms.

Length of Residence

The length of residence of ELLs in the United States is an important factor that affects their English proficiency and acculturation. The term *Generation 1.5* is used to describe some ELLs. This is because these ELLs immigrated to the United States during elementary school or high school years. They are U.S. educated but do not have English support at home; and they may be orally proficient in English but do not have adequate academic English proficiency (Li, 2015; NCELA, 2020). These ELLs may have diverse educational experiences and a wide range of language proficiency and literacy skills. In a literal sense, they are caught between generations (i.e., they belong to neither the first generation nor the second generation of immigrants). That is why they are defined by the term *Generation 1.5*.

In comparison to U.S.-born ELLs, they bring with them the characteristics from their home country but continue their assimilation and socialization in the new country. Generation 1.5 ELLs are often characterized as having a combination of new and old cultural traditions. Depending on their age at the time of immigration, the community into which they settle, the extent of education in their native country, along with some other factors, Generation 1.5 ELLs identify with their countries of origin in varying degrees. Yet this identification is also affected by their experiences growing up in the new country. These ELLs are usually bilingual and are more easily assimilated into the local culture and society than adult immigrants such as their parents.

Although some ELLs are immigrants coming with their families to the United States, many ELLs are born in the United States. A growing number of ELLs are, in fact, U.S. born (Li, 2015; NCELA, 2020). These U.S.-born ELLs may have lived in America for many years in households where caretakers speak a language other than English. English may be the dominant language for these ELLs, but they may not have developed the academic English skills and vocabulary needed to function successfully at grade level in English-speaking environments. They are also likely to suffer the same achievement gaps as Generation 1.5 ELLs because they are also from a home where no English-language support is available.

However, as the second generation of the immigrants, these U.S.-born ELLs do have some advantages in overcoming the academic challenges because they emerge into an English-speaking context at an early age of their schooling. With the proper support from teachers, educators, and policy-makers to implement high-quality early educational support programs, such as appropriate dual-language or ESOL programs, and with good assessments, these U.S.-born ELLs have the potential to do better in school than other ELLs.

Literacy Skills in the Primary Language and Previous Schooling

Literacy skills in the primary language and previous schooling can affect ELLs as they learn English and academic content knowledge, especially for those Generation 1.5 ELLs who came to the United States with their families. Even if an ELL is U.S. born, he or she may face the same challenge. For example, young ELLs in the primary grades must acquire the initial literacy concepts and skills through the medium of English, a language that they have not mastered orally before their schooling because they may not have the emergent literacy support at their non-English-speaking home environments.

Some ELLs may have developed literacy and academic skills in their home language(s). For these ELLs, the major challenge is that they must learn to read in English. Once they know how to read in English, they can transfer their L1 skills to the L2 skills. Yet some ELLs may have not experienced consistent previous schooling or appropriate instruction in the primary language(s). This compounds the difficulties because they must learn to read and write in English when they also face the challenge of learning academic content knowledge at the same time.

Some ELLs may already know some English if they arrive in the United States with strong literacy skills in the home language and adequate previous schooling. For these students, they usually grasp the concepts more easily in the L2 context than other ELLs, and they are likely to become high achievers in schools.

In addition to literacy skills in the primary language, ELLs may have an L1 that is totally different from English in language structure, word order, sound system, and word formation (Li, 2015; NCELA, 2020). For example, some ELLs' L1 may greatly differ from English in a nonalphabetic writing system (e.g., Chinese), in alphabets (e.g., Russian), or in directionalities (e.g., Hebrew). Other ELLs' home languages may be similar to English in these respects. For instance, Spanish, French, and Portuguese have more common features with English than do Swahili and Vietnamese.

Some ELLs may have an L1 that shares commonalties with English in the usage of the Roman alphabet or grammar (e.g., Italian and Polish). Other ELLs may have an L1 that shares even cognate words with English. For example, many words in English and Spanish are cognates, such as: *observe* vs. *observar*, *anniversary* vs. *aniversario*, *stomach* vs. *estómago*. Similarities between ELLs' home languages and English will make learning English easier, while differences tend to make the process more difficult.

Education of Parents, SES Status, and Resources Available at Home

The education of parents, socioeconomic status (SES), and resources available at home are also factors that affect ELLs' acquisition of L2 skills and academic content knowledge. The ELL parents' education does affect the ELLs' learning of English and literacy. Research has shown that parents' education in fact has a long-term effect on children's learning and academic success, and that the mother's level of education is an especially important factor that influences children's reading levels and school achievement (Li, 2015; NCELA, 2020). Studies also have found that the parents' education can predict the quality of family interactions and child behavior, and it further shapes, by late adolescence, educational achievement and aspirations for future educational and occupational success of their children.

SES status can often predict available resources at home associated with school attainment. Many ELLs are likely from families with lower SES conditions to afford needed learning resources that support family literacy. This can affect school performance for ELLs (Li, 2015; NCELA, 2020).

Research also has shown that some ELL parents with a lower educational background face barriers to supporting their children's schooling. These barriers include an inability to understand English, an unfamiliarity with the school system, and differences in cultural norms and cultural capital. Some ELL parents may have significant communication challenges that impact their lives and that of their children. When teachers try to involve parents in their children's learning, these barriers may limit parents' school participation.

However, research also has indicated that ELL parents do have a desire to participate in and support their children's education (Li, 2015; NCELA, 2020). Thus, educators must ensure appropriate communication between the school and parents and find ways to communicate with ELL parents in order to increase their school participation. The following are some good communication techniques to involve ELL parents:

- Have an interpreter involved in school meetings with parents so that immediate communication is available to reduce misunderstanding.
- Translate frequently used school documents for ELL parents, such as an invitation letter, the meeting schedule, and other documents.
- Provide ELL parents with choices, such as using nonverbal feedback, to make the communication easier in order to improve their participation.

- Use a telephone conference with an interpreter in the conference meetings with ELL parents if they are unable to come due to transportation.
- Use technology-based media (e.g., website and internet techniques) with easy and reliable access so that ELL parents can participate.
- Encourage ELL parents' participation by offering them opportunities, such as working with their children on some class projects.

Life Experiences and Cultural Norms

The life experiences and cultural norms also affect ELLs when they learn English and literacy. For example, Generation 1.5 ELLs, especially those who are Latino, may come from a cultural background that places a primary importance on family values. The family may expect children to take greater priority over work instead of school in times of financial needs. As a result, some ELLs may have to drop out of school to help their parents and support their family due to financial necessity.

In one case study, Amy was an example, and she sacrificed her time for school work to take care of her younger siblings and help her parents with family duties instead of focusing solely on her academic work. In Amy's own words, it was her responsibility to help her parents and support the family. Or they would have no way to survive if the parents did not work.

These ELLs bring with them not only different life experiences but also cultural norms that may have shaped their notions of appropriate teacher-student relationships. For example, the ELLs from some cultures may have learned to show respect for adults by listening quietly instead of asking questions or displaying knowledge by volunteering answers. Some ELL students may desire closeness with their teachers through physical proximity and hugs, while others may expect a more formal or distant relationship with their teachers.

Refugee ELLs may be in a more unique situation. The Geneva Convention defines a refugee as a person who, owing to fear of persecution or due to war, violence, or natural disaster, is forced outside the country of his or her nationality, and seeks refuge or asylum (Li, 2015; United Nations High Commissioner for Refugees [UNHCR], 2020). Since 1980, when the formal U.S. refugee resettlement began, 1.8 million refugees have been invited to live in the United States, with annual refugee arrivals typically between 40,000 to 75,000. These ELLs have not only limited English proficiency but also some constraints unique to this population. For example, they may have limited financial resources or a tendency to self-eliminate, or may be suffering from grief, anxiety, depression, guilt, or symptoms of post-traumatic stress disorder.

Compared to other ELLs, refugee ELLs are more likely to have difficulties with school work and adjustment issues related to these facts:

- Their education may be interrupted or postponed due to war in their home country or a waiting period of settlement in a refugee camp.
- They are faced with a sudden, unexpected transition to a new culture and new country, which may create confusion, difficulty, or uncertainty for them; it is thus difficult for them to adjust to school codes of conduct.
- These ELLs may have a sense of loss and trauma that could be profound for them; for instance, the loss may include family members or personal property, which can have psychological and emotional impacts.
- The family business in the home country may be left unsettled after leaving in a hurry; thus, basic needs and requirements such as food, housing, and immediate medical and dental care may be an urgent issue.
- They may have no parents or family guardians and experience some dramatic emotional and physical difficulties, or returning home is not an option for them.

Educators need to be sensitive to support the needs of these and all ELLs in order to help them succeed emotionally and academically. Due to the differences in the life experiences and cultural norms that ELLs bring with them, it is up to teachers to adjust teaching approaches and learning environments to accommodate the needs of ELLs and all students.

ACADEMIC ACHIEVEMENT DATA

Finally, achievement data provide facts that educators need to know. Research has shown that ELLs generally have fallen behind their English-speaking peers, and the achievement gap has persisted in the past several decades. For example, Hispanic students are outperformed by Caucasian students, though data have shown that scores have gone up for both groups in mathematics (Li, 2015; Li & Peters, 2018; National Assessment of Educational Progress [NAEP], 2020; NCES, 2020).

At the fourth-grade level, the average mathematics score for Caucasian students increased by 249 points and Hispanic students by 229 points. Yet Hispanic students still lagged behind their Caucasian peers by about the same amount compared to the scores of 20 years ago. This means that the achievement gap has not been changed in the past 20 years, and it is noticeable that over 70% of ELLs are Hispanic. Hispanic students are also less likely to complete high school, with a graduation rate of 53% for Hispanic students and 75% for Caucasian students.

It is important that teachers know their ELLs so that they can be more understanding when working work with them. This chapter discussed characteristics and types of ELLs (e.g., Generation 1.5 vs. U.S.-born ELLs). The factors that affect ELLs' learning are described, including length of residence in the United States, literacy skills in the primary language(s)/previous schooling, the educational background of parents, socioeconomic status and the resources available at home, and personal life experiences and cultural norms. Academic data are also addressed.

To help improve ELLs' learning, teachers must also practice communication skills in order to reach ELLs and their parents. Educators must be willing to share time, be encouraging, and be sensitive to the needs of refugees and all ELLs to help them achieve academic success.

REFERENCES

Li, N. (2015). *A book for every teacher: Teaching English Language Learners.* Information Age Publishing.

Li, N., & Peters, A. (2018). Promise of a democratic society: Preparing preservice teachers for the under-served ELLs. *Teacher Education Journal of South Carolina. 11*(2), 37–48.

National Assessment of Educational Progress. (2020). *NAEP report card: 2019 NAEP mathematics assessment.* Retrieved from https://nces.ed.gov/nationsreportcard

National Center for Education Statistics. (2020). *The condition of education 2020* (NCES 2020–144). U.S. Department of Education.

National Clearinghouse for English Language Acquisition. (2020). *Demographics & state data: Facts sheets.* https://ncela.ed.gov/fact-sheets#

United Nations High Commissioner for Refugees. (2020). Students from refugee backgrounds: A guide for teachers and schools. *Convention and Protocol Relating to the Status of Refugees (UNHCR).* Ministry of Education.

Chapter 13

A Need for Taiwanese Indigenous Immigrant Literature

Hsiao-Ching Lin and Antonette Aragon

To evoke social change, curricular materials for English language learners (ELLs) require various types of literature that express immigrant, multicultural, and multilingual identities of ELLs while exploring the complex understandings of each group. One way to elicit social change via curricular materials for ELLs is to examine the simplified categories of ELLs and create literature that introduces a group that has been underrepresented and not yet discussed in myriads of immigrant literature in the United States—in this case, Taiwanese indigenous immigrants.

Studies in immigrant literature (e.g., Gu, 2017; Ng, 1998) have lacked a comprehensive representation of ELLs in the United States regarding Taiwanese immigrants. The term *Taiwanese immigrants/Americans* has been predominantly claimed to refer to a group of Chinese descendants. In particular, discussions about immigrants to the United States from Taiwan (wherein the current ethnically Chinese government has imposed its settler-colonialism for over 70 years) have exclusively articulated Chinese narratives.

This chapter empirically explores some studies and curricular materials in immigrant literature and multicultural/multilingual education while offering critical autoethnographic lenses from the authors, who are a Taiwanese indigenous American and a Latina/Chicana/Mexicana American. The critical autoethnographic perspectives from the authors critique how, due to some immigrant literature, studies have considered Taiwanese peoples' ideologies and identities ought to derive from only Chinese cultures, ethnicity, and language, thus ignoring Taiwanese indigenous peoples' distinct cultures, ideologies, identities, and languages.

Decolonizing methodology is fundamental to helping expound the authors' critical perspective to resist the dominant voice that portrays Taiwanese immigrants and/or Americans through a colonial Chinese-ness. It assists this chapter in "revealing underlying texts" (Smith, 2012, p. 3) and reclaiming an *indigenous space* that is forced to *non-exist*. The indigenous space needed to be reclaimed is to recognize how the nonexistent immigrant literature is in relationship to Taiwanese indigenous immigrants in the United States.

Overall, the authors explore how ELLs could foster social change via a new recognition of literature by asking the following questions: (1) How have studies categorized Taiwanese peoples using extant literature? (2) Which studies address Taiwanese indigenous immigrant peoples' experiences in the extant literature? and (3) How could the experiences of Taiwanese indigenous immigrants help create literature or curricular materials for ELL education?

IMMIGRANT LITERATURE IN THE UNITED STATES

The marginalization and racialization of immigrant ELL students has been widespread throughout educational history. Such marginalization occurs in public education when ELL students do not have educational access to obtain curriculum proficiency. For instance, heritage Spanish-speaking students are often in schools where educators, staff, administrators, counselors, and teachers utilize deficit pedagogical praxes and perspectives of language diversity as a form of disability.

Thus, Latinx students are overrepresented in special education classes, prohibiting their educational success (Arredondo et al., 2014; Nieto & Bode, 2018; Theoharis & O'Toole, 2011). If educators desire to promote critical social justice change, inclusive education must promote services where "valuing students learning English and positioning them and their families, languages, and cultures as central . . . [are] integral aspects of the school community" (Theoharis & O'Toole, 2011, pp. 648–649).

This also means that outdated segregated pullout and separate ESL classrooms and services must be eliminated (Nieto & Bode, 2018; Theoharis & O'Toole, 2011). School leaders promoting authentic inclusivity recognize the community cultural wealth (Yosso, 2005) that ELL students bring to their education through the asset of their first-language knowledge.

Research confirms that immigrant ELL students thrive when their cultural and language differences are acknowledged, valued, and respected (Nieto & Bode, 2018; Theoharis & O'Toole, 2011; Yosso, 2005). Yet much of the research focuses on Spanish-speaking students, and it is necessary to expand the literature and focus on immigrants rendered "invisible," such as Taiwanese indigenous students.

A Need for Taiwanese Indigenous Immigrant Literature 111

Another issue that needs social change in immigrant literature from multicultural and multilingual studies is to recognize the underrepresentation of Taiwanese indigenous immigrant narratives in the studies. The issue has caused the invisibility and silence of Taiwanese indigenous immigrant narratives, thus making colonial Chinese-ness emotionally, ethnically, culturally, and linguistically claim the "Taiwanese."

Ng (1998) described who Taiwanese Americans are:

> Since immigration law changes in 1965, the Chinese population in the United States has increased dramatically. According to the 1990 U.S. Census, there were 1,645,472 Chinese Americans. While this group includes the American-born Chinese, it also encompasses those who have migrated from Hong Kong, China, Southeast Asia, Taiwan, and other parts of the world. Taiwanese Americans, the immigrants from Taiwan and their descendants, are a prominent group in this growing Chinese population. . . . Aside from the aborigines, the population on Taiwan is Chinese. They speak Mandarin Chinese, which is based on the Beijing dialect and is taught in the schools and universities on Taiwan as *guoyu* or the "national dialect." (pp. 1–5)

The definition above employed a linguistic form to formalize Chinese descendants as "Taiwanese" while Ng (1998) elaborated on the Taiwanese immigrant, families, religions, festivals, Taiwanese identity, and Taiwanese American legacy in the United States via Chinese Confucius cultivation, Chinese Alumni associations, Chinese Buddhism/Christianity/Daoism/Confucianism, and the identity conflicts with the mainlanders, in effect, distinguishing them from Chinese and from China.

Taiwanese "aborigines" are set aside from this proclamation of *Taiwanese Americans* in the United States by a more sentimental Chinese story:

> One of the factors contributing to a Taiwanese identity is its conflict with the mainlanders [Chinese people from China]. At the end of World War II, the Chinese government governed by the Nationalist Party took Taiwan back from Japan [while the Communist party won the China land during the Chinese Civil War]. The island [Taiwan—in Southeast of China mainland] had been lost during the Sino-Japanese War of 1894–95 and ceded under the terms of the Treaty of Shimonoseki of 1895. But as Chinese government officials and soldiers returned to Taiwan, tensions between the mainlanders [the Chinese Communist Party] and the Taiwanese [the Chinese Nationalist Party] mounted. (Ng, 1998, p. 104)

Ng (1998) did not show the complexity of history when writing, "The Chinese Nationalist Part took Taiwan back from Japan" (p. 104). The word *back* should be questioned; by using the word *back*, Ng (1998) ethnically and politically claimed that Taiwan's sovereignty belongs to the Chinese without mentioning the settler-colonial polity of the Chinese Nationalist Party in Taiwan.

Other aspects to consider are ways to not monopolize the term *Taiwanese immigrants/Americans*; however, literature in the United States about Taiwanese immigrants/Americans has been focused on discussing Chinese descendants without including Taiwanese indigenous peoples, who are the First Peoples of the island and whose original cultures, ethnicities, languages, religions, and customs are closer to Polynesians than to the Chinese. There is also a small group of Taiwanese indigenous peoples who have immigrated to the United States. After all, the question is, *Who has the indigeneity to own the term* Taiwanese?

As documenting the resistance about any immigrant groups' tenacity could be considered a sacred multicultural effort, the other question that ought to be pondered is, *Who has the indigeneity to own the Taiwanese resistance in U.S. immigrant literature?* Whether obliviously, purposefully, or inadvertently, referring to Taiwanese immigrants and/or Taiwanese Americans as merely the Chinese has culturally made a group of Taiwanese indigenous immigrants invisible in the U.S. literature, thus pushing them into a place where they cannot own their indigeneity as Taiwanese.

Gu (2017) successfully and affectively documented Taiwanese immigrants' resistance via their suffering, dignity, self-search, tenacity, and gender issues by depicting the international gendered domestic labor migration in the United States in the 1980s. Her book *The Resilient Self* (2017) might inadvertently accentuate the emotional legitimation of how the term *Chinese-ness* could claim the term *Taiwanese immigrants/Americans*. With the following sentiment, Taiwanese indigenous immigrant narratives might have become silent:

> Contemporary studies of gender and immigration have rarely addressed the deepest human yearning and questioning in the process of settlement: Who am I? Am I still the person I was before immigration? What has changed about me and what has not as a result of immigration? What caused these changes and how? Where is my place in the new land? How should I behave as an immigrant? (Gu, 2017, loc. 221)

In brief, she connected Chinese women who encounter discrimination in the United States as housewives with their Chinese families and their Chinese identities by claiming them to be *Taiwanese immigrants*, thus ignoring a fact that there might be other groups of Taiwanese immigrants' stories of discrimination in the United States that might not be entirely identified as Chinese only. Doing this, she fell into a trap that misclaims "Taiwanese Americans" through merely identifying all participants as "Chinese" suffering in the United States without such distinguished identities as Taiwanese indigenous.

MULTICULTURAL/MULTILINGUAL STUDIES IN THE EYES OF A TAIWANESE INDIGENOUS WOMAN

Literature in multicultural education textbooks and multilingual studies in the United States need to include Taiwanese indigenous immigrant narratives/descriptions because this group has been invisible in the immigrant literature due to dominant descriptions of Taiwanese immigrants/Americans as Chinese descendants.

As a Taiwanese indigenous immigrant woman in the United States, an ELL, and a teacher of English as a foreign/second language for over 10 years, the first author has immersed herself in the literature of critical multicultural education and multilingual studies. She has found that studies in multilingual issues regarding ELL linguistic challenges have exclusively researched Taiwanese immigrants' experiences in the context of Chinese cultures and languages. This may benefit the majority of Taiwanese immigrant/American ELLs; however, this lacks a complex representation of Taiwanese immigrants.

McKay and Wong (1996) studied four adolescent Taiwanese immigrants (termed "Chinese immigrants") and illustrated the discourse of power in their environment and their multiple and contradictory identities by exploring their English as ELLs and their use of the Chinese language. This type of study tends to simplify the ELL population of the Taiwanese immigrants/Americans as merely the Chinese by the intersectional Chinese and English identities.

Multicultural education textbooks have been dedicated to providing various sociopolitical contexts of multicultural education in the United States by trying to represent all immigrant groups' experiences. Nieto and Bode (2018) contributed to multicultural education by discussing the necessity of ELL education and making efforts to define various immigrant groups in a complex context. Specifically, they shared a Cambodian American's desire to express her cultural differences from generalized Asian American immigrant cultures such as the Japanese American, the Korean American, and the Chinese American.

In "I Am Not Asian, I Am Cambodian," Nieto and Bode (2018) presented a Cambodian American perspective that explicitly disclosed the political struggles that caused the Cambodian diaspora in the 1970s. This experience was distinguished from other realms of the Asian diaspora. With this, Nieto and Bode (2018) sent a message that multicultural and multilingual education for ELLs should strive to convey in-depth descriptions of immigrant groups by beginning to capture various silhouettes of these groups, especially for the marginalized.

However, there is also room for Nieto and Bode (2018) to include more immigrant narratives as a multicultural and multilingual education textbook, as well as ELL curricular materials. Can the Taiwanese indigenous immigrants/Americans' experiences, in the future, also be included in Taiwanese immigrant and/or American literature or the ELL curricular materials?

Seeing the underrepresentation or, suffice to say, "zero representation" of the Taiwanese indigenous immigrant group in the literature, this chapter serves to confirm this literature gap and calls for more exploration of Taiwanese indigenous immigrant narratives and stories in the United States. Specifically, the first author will conduct future research with a group of Taiwanese indigenous immigrant women from Colorado, Utah, and Washington.

POSSIBLE LITERATURE FOR ELL CURRICULAR MATERIALS

This chapter describes how the Chinese settler-colonial culturalism possesses the term *Taiwanese immigrants/Americans* in the United States and makes Taiwanese indigenous immigrants unable to claim their Taiwanese indigeneity in the United States through the term. This possession portrayed in written words unravels how Chinese colonial "civilization" in Taiwan practices cultural genocide of indigenous peoples (Wolfe, 2006) through cultural superiority, emotional advocacy for the immigrants, ethnic definitions in the literature, and ELL linguistic comparison in the United States.

Can the Taiwanese indigenous Americans/immigrants also own the term *Taiwanese* in the U.S. literature? Or should another term be used to refer to them, *the Taiwanese indigenous immigrants*? Along with the chapter's explanations, these questions may recalibrate who owns the term *Taiwanese immigrants/Americans*. These questions also exemplify the potential to include Taiwanese indigenous immigrant narratives into the discourses of Taiwanese immigrants and/or Americans. Also, these questions mean that social change should happen in ELL curricular materials.

Social change in curricular materials for ELLs requires various kinds of literature that portray critical multicultural and multilingual identities of ELLs while exploring the complex understandings of each immigrant community. It is an advocacy and a demand. Social justice invokes action to equitably provide greater access to resources and change the deeply divided systems that marginalize groups.

This social change could begin at sharing and documenting the narratives, stories, and testimonies of Taiwanese indigenous immigrants living in the United States. Their narratives might integrate multiple marginalized experiences as Taiwanese indigenous peoples in Taiwan's Chinese settler-colonialism, as People of Color or immigrants in the United States, or as the Taiwanese indigenous immigrants whose identities are interwoven with struggles, adjustments, and exchanges with their multicultural/lingual and indigenous ways of knowing in the world.

The chapter calls for more studies to explore another group of Taiwanese immigrant/American storytelling outside the Chinese narratives in U.S. immigrant literature. By doing so, English Language Learners, educators, activists, administrators, or others will be offered more comprehensive and truthful ways of thinking about the Taiwanese immigrants/Americans, the indigenous of the world, and the ELL immigrants in the United States.

REFERENCES

Arredondo, P., Gallardo-Cooper, M., Delgado-Romero, E. A., & Zapata, A. L. (2014). *Culturally responsive counseling with Latinas/os*. ACA.

Gu, C.-J. (2017). *The resilient self: Gender, immigration, and Taiwanese Americans*. Rutgers University Press.

McKay, S. L., & Wong, S.-L. C. (1996). Multiple discourses, multiple identities: Investment and agency in second-language learning among Chinese adolescent immigrant students. *Harvard Educational Review, 66*(3), 577–609. https://doi.org/10.17763/haer.66.3.n47r06u264944865

Ng, F. (1998). *Taiwanese Americans*. Greenwood Press.

Nieto, S., & Bode, P. (2018). *Affirming diversity: The sociopolitical context of multicultural education* (7th ed.). Pearson.

Smith, L. T. (2012). *Decolonizing methodologies: Research and indigenous peoples* (2nd ed.). Palgrave Macmillan.

Theoharis, G., & O'Toole, J. (2011). Leading inclusive ELL: Social justice leadership for English Language Learners. *Educational Administrative Quarterly, 47*(4), 646–688. https://doi.org/10.1177/0013161X11401616

Wolfe, P. (2006). Settler colonialism and the elimination of the Native. *Journal of Genocide Research, 8*(4), 387–409. https://doi.org/10.1080/14623520601056240

Yosso, T. J. (2005). Whose culture has capital? *Race, Ethnicity and Education, 8*(1), 69–91. https://doi.org/10.1080/1361332052000341006

Chapter 14

Lessons and Transformations From the Borderlands

Preparing Educators to Support Emerging Bilinguals

Michele L. McConnell and Kelly Metz-Matthews

Increasingly, K–12 teachers and school leaders in California are called on to support students whose first language is not English or who come from varying cultural backgrounds. In fact, as of this writing, over 1.1 million students in California are considered English Learners (henceforth emerging bilinguals), while 2.6 million, or 41.5%, of students enrolled in the K–12 system in California speak a language other than English at home (California Department of Education, 2020). Considering these figures, it seems incongruous that many preservice teachers receive only one language-acquisition course as part of their teacher-preparation program.

Unless new educators happen to have backgrounds in applied linguistics (a rarity for certain), we worry that they may not be aware of the possible effects of linguistic imperialism or internalized linguicism on California's culturally and linguistically diverse students. Certainly, we suspect that they are unlikely to have been trained on critical language pedagogies, the possibility of bilingual subtraction among their students, or accentism in the classroom. Further, unless their teacher-education programs have touted the merits of culturally and linguistically responsive or sustaining pedagogies, those, too, may be enigmatic concepts to these nascent educators.

In fact, even as culturally and linguistically responsive and sustaining pedagogies are increasingly common elements of teacher-education programs, many of the critical components of these pedagogies are approached superficially in an (understandable) effort to cover as much material as is possible in a limited frame of time.

Moreover, even as these pedagogies are crucial to creating culturally sensitive classrooms where students' unique backgrounds are leveraged to their advantage, the use of these pedagogies does not imply an in-depth understanding of critical applied linguistics (or linguistics, period) on the part of teachers. We cannot help but wonder: Are preservice teachers prepared for the realities of classrooms in which the power dynamics of language acquisition play out in real time?

While some teacher-education programs are required to provide foundational instruction in teaching emerging bilinguals (and, in some cases, do a fair job of it), not all states require an English Language Learner authorization as part of the initial credentialing process. As a result, teachers and educational leaders across the United States are to some degree working in the field of English Language Development (ELD) without necessarily having trained for it. This matters, not least because, as Motha (2014) pointed out, "the English language carries enticing meaning and is connected to social advancement, opportunity, modernity, wealth, enlightenment, Whiteness, and cosmopolitanism" (p. 4).

Considering the degree to which the English language is fraught with tension and power, the disconnect between credentialing and practice is of real concern. In fact, even teachers of monolingual—but nonetheless diverse—students would benefit from a more in-depth knowledge of developmental language acquisition and the multitude of forms of literacy. After all, students' literacies can have an outsized impact on their long-term educational outcomes in content areas beyond English Language Arts.

Critically, as Lippi-Green (2012) suggests, myths around literacy play a role in the subjugation of spoken forms of language to written forms of language. This, she argues, is part of what Foucault (1972, 1977) might call *the disciplining of the discourse.*

As teacher-educators, our concern is that without some cognizance of the ways power runs through these so-called language and literacy "norms," teachers are ill-equipped to navigate such power dynamics in their classrooms. And we are not the only ones to express this concern. Research from the field (see Anstrom et al., 2010; Cadiero-Kaplan & Rodriguez, 2008; Takanishi & Le Menestrel, 2017) has suggested that for these and other reasons, K–12 teachers and leaders are not necessarily always prepared to support culturally and linguistically diverse learners even as the use of culturally and linguistically responsive and sustaining pedagogies are on the uptick.

As teacher-educators in the borderlands of California, we are increasingly concerned that our preservice teachers lack the preparation necessary to navigate linguistically diverse classrooms in meaningful ways. Alas, without initiating a complete program redesign around applied linguistics, what could be done to prepare them to navigate the power dynamics and realities of the English language in borderlands classrooms? To that end, one of us designed a short-term elective course in Mexicali, Mexico, to support teachers in growing their social and critical consciousness.

Offered for 3 consecutive years, we hoped it would better prepare preservice teachers to create effective and safe learning environments for emerging bilinguals. In designing the course, we hoped to explore whether, through short-term immersive study in the borderlands of Mexico, teachers without backgrounds in critical applied linguistics might come to more in-depth understandings of the linguistic needs and realities of students. In other words, could a course of this type fill part of the gaping hole we had identified in teacher education and thereby help teachers better support emerging bilinguals in their eventual classrooms?

Beginning in 2014 and ending in 2018, the course took preservice teachers, teacher leaders, and TESOL graduate students to visit and teach in a variety of public and private elementary and secondary schools across Mexicali, Mexico; they also listened to several teacher- and administrator-led panels and visited local museums, charities, crisis centers, deportation shelters, and various community and neighborhood organizations central to the educational experiences of many Mexican children and families.

Pre- and post-travel work included the exploration of social location, readings on the Mexican educational system, discussions of language's role in ameliorating or sustaining inequities, personal reflection essays about the coursework, an opportunity to teach English as a second language in a university-based language department, and case study work on one aspect related to teaching emerging bilinguals in U.S. classrooms.

THE STUDY

The purpose of this chapter is to examine the results of a mixed-methods study into the effects of the course, with particular attention paid to the role of social positionality exploration as a focal point of teacher preparation. The 35 participants in the course identified primarily as preservice teachers, but also included select teacher leaders and TESOL graduate students.

As a framework for analysis, we utilized the four queries set out in Zaytoun's (2006) work on theorizing at the borders: (1) the personal as political, (2) the political as personal, (3) the connection between personal consciousness, social consciousness, and political activism, and (4) the relationship between the growth of personal and social consciousness as a result of living with the tensions of varying social locations. This framework provides context for the specific benefits that participants experienced from their work on social location during the course.

The exploration of social location is a way to discover how our socially constructed identities, agency, and social responsibilities and actions connect and emerge over time in relation to context (Zaytoun, 2006). Freire (1970) has long suggested that education is itself a political act, and Zaytoun's framework adds context by demonstrating how understanding one's social location invariably affects teachers' biases, perceptions, and interactions with students, specifically emerging bilinguals.

DISCUSSION OF FINDINGS

In what follows, we pay special attention to one of the most salient themes of our research—namely that immersive study in the borderlands coupled with reflective pedagogy on social location led to perceptions of transformation on the part of participants. Preservice teachers felt the coursework positively impacted their ability to take up inclusive forms of teaching and leadership within various educational situations, particularly in the context of multilingual schools and classrooms. To that end, we provide examples of how current teachers, teacher-educators, and administrators might incorporate social positionality into professional development and their classrooms as a means of helping new teachers become better aware of the differentiated needs of their culturally and linguistically diverse students.

Acknowledging We Are Part of a Larger System

Prior to traveling to Mexicali, preservice teachers engaged in Deardorff's "Identity Tag Game" (2012b) and "Using the Intercultural Competence Process Model" (from 2012a) as mechanisms for support in exploring constructions of self and identity. During the identity tag game, preservice teachers listed their various identities and wrote a reflective statement about the identity they felt was most salient. Out of 35 reflections, 32 reported that their most salient identity was created based on their hard work and effort (e.g., graduate student, teacher, athlete) while only three noted the connection to relationships which supported or created a shared identity (e.g., parental encouragement, employer reference letter, mentor).

Additionally, no preservice teacher related their identities to a greater system of privilege or politics, exemplifying a lack of connection to Freire's (1970) notion of critical consciousness. This exposes that those entering the field of education may not have considered and/or acknowledged the relationships that grant them access to their current identities as teachers and graduate students. To connect the personal to the political, one must acknowledge the interplay of relationships between the self and others as a means of growth and development (Zaytoun, 2006). A lack of consciousness of these relationships on the part of preservice teachers is one of several factors in sustaining the myth of meritocracy.

The second pre-travel activity, Deardorff's (2012a) "Using the Intercultural Competence Process Model," posits that gaining intercultural competence is a process between an individual and various interactions that builds knowledge and impacts attitudes toward a culture other than one's own. For intercultural competence to occur, one must practice critical self-reflection upon attitudes and experiences which challenge one's personal perspectives (Deardorff, 2012a).

Using a Likert Scale self-reflection tool designed by Deardorff (2012a), preservice teachers rated themselves in the following areas: (1) respecting and valuing other cultures, (2) openness to learning from different cultures, (3) tolerance for ambiguity, empathy, (4) cultural self-awareness, and (5) understanding others' worldviews. Interestingly, pre-travel scores showed that 95% of the preservice teachers ranked themselves as high or very high in those aspects of intercultural competence.

Post-travel, preservice teachers participated in two final class sessions in which they reflected on their initial identity tag game documents and intercultural competence surveys. In that exercise, 90% of the preservice teachers noted that the identities they chose to share initially were not ones they felt were "substantive" to who they are; rather, they noted, their initial identities were aligned with socially accepted identities within American culture.

Also of note, 95% of the preservice teachers indicated that meaningful identities—those that helped them connect and communicate in Mexicali— were identities created through relationships such as daughter, friend, and mother. Finally, 86% of preservice teachers shared that their identities as graduate students, teachers, and leaders were "political." According to one preservice teacher, they "connect to the privileges of our experiences and relationships afforded within the system."

In returning to the intercultural competence survey, preservice teachers admitted to social desirability bias as they reflected on their reactions and actions in Mexicali. Upon their return, preservice teachers were more open to sharing their lack of tolerance, lack of flexibility, and inability to withhold judgment in post-travel courses.

Zaytoun (2006) noted that beginning to understand that all people have changing identities and perspectives as experienced from varying social locations begins to dismantle fixed socially constructed identities such as race, gender, and language. This transformation of thought allowed preservice teachers to recognize their connection to the political. In other words, the course allowed preservice teachers to see themselves in relation to how they see others.

Getting to the Political Is Personal

Zaytoun (2006) offered three perspectives for analyzing how the political is connected to personal consciousness: outsider-within (Collins, 2000), borderland/Conocimiento (Anzaldua, 1999), and privilege. To support preservice teachers' ability to explore their positionality and grow their critical consciousness, they wrote and shared a social location essay.

In the essay, the graduate students outlined their social location beginning with their family of origin to the present, exploring how their social location might enhance or disrupt their professional and personal work, especially regarding their ability to identify and intervene around conflict or violence. As part of that process, they defined what violence and conflict within education might look, sound, or feel like.

Arellano and colleagues (2016) named 10 deficit myths held about Latina/o children that teachers need to interrogate and transform. In the preservice teachers' social location essays, 5 of the 10 deficit myths were identified:

1. Latino/a students don't do well in school due to poverty;
2. Latino/a parents don't care and can't read; therefore, they don't help their children with school;
3. English guarantees future success;
4. Early bilingualism leads to slower growth in both languages; and
5. These beliefs and ideologies were not seen as deficits, as they were considered "facts" and would impact teaching practices.

During the trip, a turning point was acknowledged by the preservice teachers. In a rural town outside Mexicali, preservice teachers were asked by locals to teach an English lesson involving conversational English on how to sell honey and how to add and subtract using U.S. dollars. While the local community relied heavily on honey sales for survival, American preservice teachers were initially upset by both the request and level of poverty they identified in the community.

During the trip, preservice teachers learned that poverty within the community was created by changes in housing fire codes within California and Arizona. The community used to make and sell roof tiles, from which they made a better living; when fire codes changed, their income dropped. While still in Mexicali, one student commented, "Can you believe they want us to teach how to sell honey? English should be for improving one's position in life. Like grammar and reading." Another preservice teacher commented,

"I'm offended that all they want children to do is work for the family. They just don't get it."

During a post-travel class reflection on the incident, preservice teachers admitted a need to identify with a political identity:

> I just went with the story I've been taught. English will take you places, like college. We need English for improving our lives. In the moment, I was like selling honey versus going to college. Like I didn't even realize that the parents are teaching a life skill: maintaining a business. Selling honey includes science, math, and speaking. Skills needed to survive. Like how we survive depends on our situation in life. It really is the funds of knowledge that we read about in other classes in action.

In response, another preservice teacher added that she is now continually questioning her beliefs about language and language acquisition, "I'm questioning everything I ever believed about English and abilities and realizing some of it is lies."

Living With Tensions and Challenges

When we change ourselves, we change the world around us (Anzaldua, 1983; Collins, 1998; Zaytoun, 2006). As our personal consciousness transforms into a critical personal consciousness, we are more likely to move into action as we transform our practices and engage with the world around us differently. Those preservice teachers who were willing to dig into their personal identities and critically reflect on their stories in light of their experiences in Mexicali came to see a system of power that creates and supports inaccuracies and harmful myths.

Preservice teachers who recently participated in the course reported deepening their connection to a social consciousness as a result of their learnings in the course. They reported reading books by bell hooks, Gholdy Muhammad, Gloria Anzaldua, Angela Valenzuela, and Paulo Freire. They also reported reconnecting to the arts via CECUT (Centro Cultural Tijuana) and forming a group in which they visit local Tijuana coffee shops and build community while learning more about La Frontera and border culture. Finally, several students reported traveling more, as "the world has so much to offer my classroom."

Those preservice teachers who participated in earlier offerings of the course discussed a commitment to growing critical consciousness for themselves while helping others to do the same even when it meant "living with tensions." As one preservice teacher, now a school director, shared when asked about systemic barriers for bilingual students: "I can't not see it now, but I continue to need to know more to help my teachers."

Other past course participants shared that they are implementing counter-narratives in the classroom and with families, enacting critical pedagogies, practicing action research and critical reflection, and letting go of myths regarding bilingual students. Yet that final action (letting go of long-held myths) continues to be a struggle; according to one preservice teacher, there is "this constant tension between how we test, what we test, who we test, and how we share the test data."

Prior to designing the course in Mexicali, we wondered whether preservice teachers were prepared for classrooms, especially those in the borderlands, in which the power dynamics of language acquisition play out in real time. Admittedly, we (like others before us) were not convinced that they were prepared absent advanced training in critical applied linguistics. But could a short-term immersive course change that, and, if so, to what degree? Could we offer preservice teachers, in at least some small measure, some of the tools required to better understand themselves and their emerging bilingual students in the context of education in the borderlands?

This study suggests that, yes, some of the glaring gaps in teacher preparation can be filled through deliberate work around social positionality exploration and the development of critical consciousness. Our research offers that without additional coursework or in-depth guided critical reflections, the myth of meritocracy and deficit myths regarding culturally and linguistically diverse K–12 students and their families will continue. These myths are deeply embedded within a culture of individualism and assimilation practices. If we are properly preparing preservice teachers to work with emerging bilinguals, we cannot afford for those myths to remain embedded in the broader systems in which we are all, wittingly or not, suspended.

As the preservice teachers in the study learned, we must fully know ourselves and the culture in which we teach before we can begin to build political awareness and identity. One course on language acquisition is not enough for preservice teachers to understand internalized linguicism, accentism, and how cultural beliefs impact potential acts of bilingual subtraction. Furthering learning about critical language pedagogies within and across teacher-education programs and professional development opportunities does support teachers as they move beyond the superficial understandings of creating culturally and linguistically safe classrooms.

Teacher educators and leaders may want to consider infusing coursework or professional development with intercultural competencies (see Deardorff, 2012a), critical self-reflection (see Arellano et al., 2016), and implementation of the identity framework provided by Zaytoun (2006) to evaluate pre- and in-service teachers' critical cultural growth.

REFERENCES

Anstrom, K., DiCerbo, P., Butler, F., Katz, A., Millet, J., & Rivera, C. (2010). *A review of the literature on academic English: Implications for K–12 English Language Learners.* The George Washington University Center for Equity and Excellence in Education.

Anzaldua, G. E. (1983). La preita. In G. E. Anzaldua & C. Moraga (Eds.), *The bridge called me back: Writings by radical women of color* (pp. 198–209). Kitchen Table Women of Color Press.

Anzaldua, G. E. (1999). *Borderlands/La frontera: The new mestiza.* Aunt Lute Books.

Arellano, A., Cintrón, J., Flores, B., & Berta-Ávila, M. (2016). Teaching for critical consciousness: Topics, themes, frameworks, and instructional activities. In A. Valenzuela (Ed.), *Growing critically conscious teachers: A social justice curriculum for educators of Latino/a youth* (pp. 39–66). Teachers College Press.

Cadiero-Kaplan, K., & Rodriguez, J. L. (2008). The preparation of highly qualified teachers for English language learners: Educational responsiveness for unmet needs. *Equity & Excellence in Education, 41*(3), 372–387.

California Department of Education. (2020, July 9). *Facts about English learners in California CalEdFacts.* CDE Data and Statistics. https://www.cde.ca.gov/ds/sd/cb/cefelfacts.asp

Collins, P. H. (1998). *Fighting words: Black women and the search for justice.* University of Minnesota Press.

Collins, P. H. (2000). *Black feminist thought: Knowledge, consciousness and the politics of empowerment.* Routledge.

Deardorff, D. K. (2012a). Framework: Intercultural competence model. In K. Berardo & D. K. Deardorff (Eds.), *Building cultural competence: Innovative activities and models* (pp. 45–52). Stylus.

Deardorff, D. K. (2012b). Identity tag game. In K. Berardo & D. K. Deardorff (Eds.), *Building cultural competence: Innovative activities and models* (pp. 151–157). Stylus.

Foucault, M. (1972). *The archaeology of knowledge and the discourse on language.* Pantheon.

Foucault, M. (1977). *Discipline and punish: the birth of the prison.* Penguin.

Freire, P. (1970). *Pedagogy of the oppressed.* Bloomsbury.

Lippi-Green, R. L. (2012). *English with an accent: Language, ideology, and discrimination in the United States.* Routledge.

Motha, S. (2014). *Race, empire, and English language teaching: Creating responsible and ethical anti-racist practice.* Teachers College Press.

Takanishi, R., & Le Menestrel, S. (Eds.). (2017). *Promoting the educational success of children and youth learning English: Promising futures.* The National Academies Press.

Zaytoun, K. (2006). Theorizing at the borders: Considering social location in rethinking self and psychological development. *NWSA Journal, 18*(2), 52–72.

Chapter 15

Strategies for Moving From Learning English, Bilingual Education to a More Inclusive Multilingual Education

Georgina Y. García and Jan Perry Evenstad

This chapter explores the history of how bilingual or multilingual education has evolved. People when they think of bilingual education today make assumptions that it is only for Spanish-speaking students. The authors' following discussion is grounded in how bilingual education has become associated with recent Spanish-speaking immigrants and suggests that moving toward an inclusive description is more appropriate and less politically charged.

Much of the approach in teaching students and adults for whom English is not their first language has been the sink-or-swim method, meaning that we put you in a classroom where the teacher and most students speak English and hope you will begin to learn the language. As a country we do not have an official language, and states vary in their laws in designating English as an official language. Schildkrau (2001) in her piece on "Official English and the States: Influences on Declaring English the Official Language in the United States" indicated that 26 states have declared English as the official language of their state through statutes and/or amendments to state constitutions.

This certainly can influence a state's approach to bilingual or multilingual education, as our national constitution passively gives states the right to determine their own education system. Faingold (2012) referenced states that have maintained a more "hands-off" policy like the U.S. Constitution, and "nonnativist" being more neutral or favorable of speakers of other languages. He referred to states that, through their legislative process, have made English the official language as being "hands-on" and "nativist" and seemingly unfavorable toward speakers of other languages.

Most of us have learned in elementary school about the early settlement in Virginia. We were told it was settled by the English and made the logical assumption that it was just an English settlement. According to Goldenberg and Wagner (2015), during the 17th century in Virginia, settlers included Polish immigrants, who can be linked to the beginnings of bilingual education in the colonies. They were extended the rights of Englishmen, as they had the skills for shipbuilding and glasswork that were desperately needed by the colony. This led to the Poles establishing the first bilingual schools.

Crawford (1987) noted that there were numerous Native American languages spoken, and Castellanos and Leggio (1983) put the number of native languages at about 500 during this time. While English was widespread, the 17th-century colonies had sizable enclaves of German, Dutch, French, Swedish, and Polish immigrants. Castellanos and Leggio went on to say that one of the reasons why the English Pilgrims left Holland was in part due to the fact that their children were losing their English language. Like immigrants past and present, there has always been the desire to vigorously preserve native languages and customs.

From the mid-19th century to the first half of the 20th century, there was a shift in the acceptance of bilingual education in the United States. Also, during this time, there was a great influx of immigrants from southern and eastern Europe, and many people feared that this new wave of immigration would bring with it foreign ideologies that would conflict with what was becoming American nationalism. Following the Civil War, in 1882 Congress passed the Immigration Act of 1882, which was one of the first attempts to broaden federal oversight of immigration, as some states had already passed their own immigration laws (Migration Policy Institute, 2013).

In 1906, the Naturalization Act was passed (Ovando, 2003), which required immigrants to be able to speak English to become naturalized U.S. citizens. As WWI advanced, so did the wave of nationalism, along with the belief that immigrants should become "Americans" as quickly as possible. This "Americanization," as Kober (2020) and Gándara and Escamilla (2017) mentioned, included the suppression of all languages other than English; in many cases, immigrants gave up their language, heritage, and ethnic surnames.

According to Tyack and Cuban (1995), one of the central purposes of public schooling was to assimilate the new immigrants. In 1919, according to Baker and Wright (2017), a resolution adopted by the Americanization Department of the U.S. Bureau of Education recommended that education in all public and private schools be conducted in English. The early Supreme Court case *Meyer v. Nebraska* (1923) ruled that languages other than English could not be taught in schools beyond the eighth grade (Pavlenko, 2002;

Baker et al., 2016). As Bybee and colleagues (2014) pointed out, at this time in history, the rise in language ideology, moving toward a common language, occurred alongside restrictive immigration policies, while free and compulsory education was continuing to spread.

Bybee et al. also indicated that despite the restrictive immigration policies and assimilationist efforts, many continued to speak their native languages. Recently, we have been reminded by Alvarez (2020) that language suppression and oppression are traumatic, with research showing that speaking more than one language only improves brain function and helps English learners become proficient in English.

By the late 1950s, the launching of Sputnik by Russia brought about the passage of the new National Defense Act of 1958, and the teaching of mathematics, sciences, and foreign languages became the new focus in schools. The emphasis on foreign language was in the interests of national security and safety. The push to learn languages other than English was for White students in K–12 schools. In higher education, fellowships and funding were in place for students who would become foreign language teachers (Baker et al., 2016; Ovando, 2003). The "rebirth" of bilingual education, as Ovando (2003) cited, came with Fidel Castro's Cuban Revolution in 1959.

In 1962 President John F. Kennedy signed the Migration and Refugee Assistance Act for refugees and in particular Cuban nationals fleeing communism (Migration Policy Institute, 2013). Many Cubans fled to the United States, specifically to Florida, with the hope that the revolution would be short lived and they could return back home to Cuba. While in Florida, they developed a successful two-way bilingual education program at Coral Way Elementary school in Dade County, which became a model for bilingual education (Crawford, 1987; Ovando, 2003; Goldenberg & Wagner, 2015; Gándara & Escamilla, 2017).

The 1960s, when the country began to officially recognize the civil rights of national origin students and their access and opportunity to an education, brought about many important pieces of legislation. The legislation of this time also reflected the history of the ebb and flow of learning English from a positive standpoint to one of contempt. When paralleled with the history of immigration, we see which languages are in favor at certain points of time. In 1965 President Lyndon B. Johnson signed the Immigration and Nationality Act (Wolgin, 2015), abolishing national-origin quotas and expanding entry based on family reunification.

During the Johnson era, the Bilingual Education Act of 1968 was passed. Kloss (1977) contended that the act was the first measure at the federal level to promote bilingual education. It was said that one of the contributing factors to the passage of the 1968 Bilingual Education Act was that, at one point in time, the president taught school in Cortulla, Texas, and incorporated Spanish into his instruction (Blanton, 2005; Bybee et al., 2014).

Spring (2001, 2011), a historian, reminded us that though there were political motivations behind Senator Yarborough's (Texas) support of legislation focused on Spanish-speaking students, the 1968 act's passage was also motivated by the efforts of Native Americans and Puerto Ricans who were interested in preserving their languages. Spring also pointed out that instruction involved teaching English and either Spanish or Native American languages.

The 1970 saw two major pieces of legislation that impacted bilingual education, *Lau v. Nichols* and *Castaneda v. Pickard*. Baker and Wright (2017) stated that the *Lau* case has come to symbolize the fight for language rights in the United States. As Nieto (2009) noted, the *Lau* decision mandated school districts to provide the necessary programs and accommodations for students who did not speak English. However, the ruling did not define the type of bilingual programs to be implemented but required "appropriate action."

The lack of specificity in the *Lau* decision led to the 1981 *Castaneda v. Pickard* case, which described appropriate action in implementing programs for language minority students as the following: (1) The program must be based on sound educational theory; (2) the program must have sufficient resources and personnel; and (3) the program must prove to be effective in teaching students English (Ovando, 2003; Nieto, 2009; Bybee et al., 2014; Baker et al., 2016).

Kim et al. (2015) and Gándara and Escamilla (2017) listed the following most common bilingual programs used:

1. Submersion: Instruction is entirely in English with no special language services, the old sink-or-swim approach.
2. English for Speakers of Other Languages (ESOL): This focuses on the acquisition of English language skills.
3. Bilingual: Two languages are used in the classroom—the native language and English.
4. Other: Can be known as late exit, maintenance, developmental bilingual, or any program that differs from transitional bilingual education.

Whatever program a school district chooses to implement, according to Nieto (2009), "the word 'bilingual,' beyond denoting 'speaker of two languages,' has come to symbolize an immigrant, typically a Latino or Latina, who does not—and refuse to—speak English correctly and, therefore, who cannot be considered 'American'" (Spolsky, 2004; Tollefson, 2002).

Throughout the anti-bilingual movement of the 1980s and 1990s, No Child Left Behind, and various 21st-century approaches to English language learning, we have a myriad of legislative requirements and mandates. No Child

Left Behind legislation essentially rolled back the Bilingual Education Act and put a new focus on English "acquisition" (Evans & Hornberger, 2005; Sinclair, 2018). Bilingual education is still alive and being used; some of the most common programming used today is mentioned above.

The watering down of the original Bilingual Education Act has been often attributed to sociopolitical debate around the rights of language minority students and communities and English-only narratives and supporters of such policies (Castellanos & Leggio, 1983; Crawford, 1998, 1999; Gándara et al., 2010; Ovando, 2003; Wiley, 2007; Sinclair, 2018) and has only taken from the critical thinking of programming that will serve all students learning and acquiring English. It has also left much to be desired in advocating and supporting school community languages to be used and be a part of the educational experience.

Questions to consider today are:

- Who does bilingual education serve and who does it leave out by the mere label of *bilingual education* and its historical confluence?
- Is the historical label representative of legislation and policy for all students?
- Is it time to explore the relevancy of the learning of English and its relationship to the label of *bilingual education* through the lens of inclusivity and the informal policies of how the languages of favor may not be justification for the label use today? (In fact, the label may be limiting and creating inequity within instruction and student learning.)

As stated previously, bilingual education has been part of the educational history of the United States since the 19th century. It was a normal practice throughout the country's educational landscape (Blanton, 2007; Kloss, 1998; Sinclair, 2018). Growing xenophobia and otherization began to stagnate and negatively impact bilingual education across the nation, as previously mentioned. It was not until the 1960s that activism and advocacy for federally funded bilingual educational programming appeared again, alongside the Civil Rights movement (Sinclair, 2018) and the immigration impacts of the largest guest-worker program in U.S. history: the Mexican Farm Labor Agreement, also known as the Bracero program, which created a new Mexican American community and ignited a boiling movement.

However, this programming would be a Spanish-English model that had the hopes of acclaiming cultural legacy that cultivated and enacted the linguistic capital of students and communities where Spanish was their first language and the language they navigated and used in their daily lives (Sinclair, 2018). While the 1968 Bilingual Education Act seemed to be a good theory of action—and it was the right thing to do to meet the needs of the ever-growing

Mexican American Spanish-speaking population—the sociopolitical debate and revisions and rollbacks in the following decades negatively impacted the ideal future for these students.

The evolution of this legislation has created stigma as well as otherization within education and educational practices for Latino students in the United States. The push for and constant revisions and amendments for bilingual education magnified demographic shifts, perpetuating stereotypes and prejudice against Latino students and feelings about Latino immigration that increased the resistance to the idea of serving these students (Houvouras, 2001). Not only did it spotlight Spanish-speaking students negatively, but also this approach began to erode the notion of bilingual education for all minority language groups in the United States to a focus on the Spanish-speaking community.

It also skewed the programming to students who had a narrow ability within the English language, as Sinclair (2018) pointed out, and thus labeling and defining them by a perceived incapability to speak English versus the ability to learn and acquire the English language, attributing a sense of educational impotence to these students and communities. Bilingual education became synonymous with the Mexican American and the Latino, Spanish-speaking population and their educational experience, and it still is today.

In a 2020 article, Pew Research Center reported that in 2018, 11.2 million immigrants living in the United States had come from the countries of Mexico, China—including Macao, Hong Kong, Taiwan, and Mongolia—India, the Philippines, and El Salvador (Budiman, 2020). Mexico at one point was the leading country in immigration numbers, but that has since tapered off, with more Mexicans exiting the United States to return to Mexico (Budiman, 2020). Another type of immigration to consider is the resettlement of refugees; since 1980, approximately 3 million refugees have been resettled in the United States, most originating from the Democratic Republic of the Congo, followed by Burma (Myanmar), Ukraine, Eritrea, and Afghanistan (Budiman, 2020).

Concurrently, the newest wave of immigration, according to the Migration Policy Institute (2013), is an exodus of people escaping distressed Latin American countries, such as Venezuela, Colombia, Peru, Ecuador, Chile, and Argentina. These immigration trends beg the question: Where do these students coming from countries other than Mexico fit in this Spanish/English frame of bilingual education, and what are the impacts of that frame?

Looking at this issue when it comes to students and communities from Mexico and Latin America, there is the problematic notion of creating a monolithic group in the frame of Spanish/English bilingual education. Mexico, Central, and South America are all in Latin America, which consists of 21 countries, excluding the Caribbean (Latin American Network

Information Center, n.d.), many that are represented in this exodus. But Spanish is not spoken or a dominant language in all of these countries. Some countries have their own forms of Spanish that are different from the Spanish spoken in Mexico, and countries like Brazil speak Portuguese; Central American countries have their own rich dialects and indigenous languages.

To associate being Latino or from Latin America with a Spanish/English model for bilingual education has problematic implications for these students and communities. By doing so, a monolithic narrative is created that groups all these diverse students and communities into one sole group and community. They may stand together in solidarity and advocacy, but to see them through a myopic and monolithic lens erases their individual cultures, languages, and heritages and their diverse educational needs, thus perpetuating the stereotype of being powerless in learning and acquiring the English language due to their limited language capital in English (Sinclair, 2018) and learning the language through a frame and model built for and focusing on Spanish speakers learning English.

Many of these students and communities from Latin America and other parts of the globe come to the United States already being multilingual and literate in their own languages and dialects, not knowing English or having limited English language capital.

These language-minoritized students and the communities in which they live in become victim to stereotypes and biases created by language education policies that have further perpetuated societal inequities within these communities such as poverty, racism, and xenophobia (Flores & Chaparro, 2017)—this has a long history in the United States as demographics shift— thus leading to situations of linguistic racism against these students and communities, ironically because of their linguistic attributes. Instead of creating hostile educational conditions, we need to create *transcaring* (Aguayo, 2020) conditions and environments that provide value, appreciation for primary language, and belonging for these students that is inclusive.

Seeing that these students come from countries with diverse languages, dialects, and indigenous languages, they are already multilingual before coming to the United States and entering the U.S. school system. Many of them go back and forth between languages in any given conversation and in thought even before learning English. This is a skill that is built naturally in countries that are multilingual, as opposed to the United States, which is for the most part monolingual.

De Costa (2020) espoused that linguistic racism is intensified when the person speaking is multilingual and actively goes between different languages and language patchworking. This is not seen in monolingual situations, and it is something that students and communities of color have been grappling with on a daily basis as immigrants to the United States due to their deep and expansive linguistic inventories (De Costa, 2020).

While this should be acknowledged and viewed as a resource and benefit in the learning and acquiring of English, it has been and continues to be deemed and seen as negative and shameful. This not only creates feelings and narratives of otherization for these students and communities but also starts to create a divide and total separation from other language learners who do not come from Spanish-speaking communities and/or perceived Spanish-speaking communities.

Today, immigration from Latin America and undocumented immigration in general is on the rise and is often perceived as a threat. Research has shown that when one perceives a group to be a problem to oneself or to one's experience in society or public education, it impacts their demeanor and behavior toward that group (Bobo & Hutchings, 1996; Jackman & Muha, 1984; Houvouras, 2001). This happens in educational programming, such as how bilingual programs are enacted as linguistic racism is many times carried out implicitly (De Costa, 2020), through actions, policies, procedures, practices, and how we view those who are "other" to the norm and/or majority.

Often, parents of students learning English opt out of bilingual programs because their home language is something other than Spanish, and they perceive bilingual programs to be only for Spanish-speaking students and created to meet the needs of Spanish-speaking students; or Spanish-speaking parents opt out to avoid stigma and otherization even though these students need support in acquiring the English language. Again, these actions are carried out implicitly as parents are trying to do the "best" and "right" things for their children and making decisions based on what they believe will give them a "better" opportunity and educational experience.

What are some strategies that can help these situations? Jim Cummins wrote, "Good teaching does not require us to internalize an endless list of instructional techniques. Much more fundamental is the recognition that human relationships are essential to effective instruction" (quoted in Nieto & Bode, 2018, p. 229). It starts with authentic relationships.

There is an urgent need to change the way we look at bilingual education as a whole and for educators to reframe how they meet the needs of all students, starting with the following:

1. Heal and remove the historical notion that bilingual education is synonymous with Spanish-speaking Latino students and solely for them. Instead, refer to it as multilingual education for bilingualism and biliteracy to bring a community of multilingual learners together and create what Aguayo (2020) referred to as *transcaring* environments to belong.

2. Educate teachers in teacher-preparation programs as well as in schools on intentional instructional differentiation for multilingual education versus continuing a one-size-fits-all approach through monolingual educational structures. This will be paramount in the contexts where the language and genres being practiced and used at home will not be the same as the ones that will be needed for mastery for long-term academic empowerment and achievement (White et al., 2015).
3. Build authentic relationships with students and parents to understand the long-term societal impacts and inequities of linguistic racism such as poverty, job segregation, racism, and xenophobia (to name a few) and to become language activists and practice anti-racist approaches to teaching for the success of their students from language-minoritized communities. This will create multilingual spaces of belonging throughout classrooms and entire schools that start with appreciation for the multilingual empowerment students already bring, rather than a sense of incapability or perceived powerlessness due to limited English-language capital.

Educating educators and educational leaders about how we refer to education policy and programming and the terms that we use is key. When behavior changes policies, shifts happen. The term *bilingual education* is outdated and problematically targets groups of minoritized language and racialized students. The *English Learner* or *English Language Learner* label was and is used to identify students in an unbiased way who are learning English, yet, as Aguayo (2020) described, it also carries an implicit and unintentional perceived homogeneity "among peers and teachers to socially and academically engage with EL-labeled students" (p. ii).

This notion has fueled inequitable learning experiences and opportunities not only in the short-term classroom experience but also in the long-term life experiences of students. It is imperative that we start to change the norm in how we speak about multilingual students learning English and the labels we attach, as the socioemotional and life success of their future selves and their communities depend on it.

While organizations like U.S. English continue to espouse and elevate the narrative of English as a standard language in the United States, they have publicly stated that they support the use of primary languages of students who are learning English to be used as a "technique" in classrooms (Imhoff, 1990). This is not enough to change how these students or communities are viewed, and it continues to marginalize them via language.

Many feel that multilingual education/bilingual education is a political platform; it will stop being political when the needs of every student are met equitably, and that starts with teachers, schools, and parents. The ways we refer to our students and the labels we apply to them should be inclusive and multilingual. This should guide our practice as multiculturalists in the classroom.

REFERENCES

Aguayo, V. A. (2020). *Life after the EL label: Conversations about identity, language, and race* [Unpublished doctoral dissertation]. University of San Francisco. https://repository.usfca.edu/diss/522

Alvarez, B. (2020) Linguistic discrimination still lingers in many classrooms. *NEA News*. https://www.nea.org/advocating-for-change/new-from-nea/linguistic-discrimination-still-lingers-many-classrooms

Baker, C., & Wright, W. E. (2017). *Foundations of bilingual education and bilingualism* (6th ed.). Multilingual Matters.

Baker, D. L., Basaraba, D. L., & Polanco, P. (2016). Connecting the present to the past: Furthering the research on bilingual education and bilingualism. *Review of Research in Education, 40*, 821–883.

Blanton, C. K. (2005) *The strange career of bilingual education in Texas*. Texas A&M University Press.

Bobo, L., & Hutchings, V. L. (1996). Perceptions of racial group competition: Extending Blumer's theory of group position to a multiracial social context. *American Sociological Review, 61*(6), 951. https://doi.org/10.2307/2096302

Budiman, A. (2020, August 20). *Key findings about U.S. immigrants*. Pew Research. https://www.pewresearch.org/fact-tank/2020/08/20/key-findings-about-u-s-immigrants

Bybee, E. R., Henderson, K. I., & Hinojosa, R. V. (2014). An overview of U.S. bilingual education: Historical roots, legal battles, and recent trends. *Texas Education Review, 2*(2), 138–146.

Castellanos, D., & Leggio, P. (1983). *The best of two worlds: Bilingual-bicultural education in the U.S.* Office of Equal Education Opportunity, New Jersey Department of Education.

Castañeda v. Pickard. 648 F. 2d 989 (5th Cir. 1981).

Crawford, J. (1987). Bilingual education traces its U.S. roots to the colonial era. *Education Week, 6*(27). https://www.edweek.org/ew/articles/1987/04/01/27early.h06.html?PageSpeed=noscript

Crawford, J. (1998). What now for bilingual education. *Rethinking Schools, 13*(2), 1.

Crawford, J. (1999). *Bilingual education: History, politics, theory and practice*, 4th ed. Bilingual Education Services.

De Costa, P. I. (2020). Linguistic racism: Its negative effects and why we need to contest it. *International Journal of Bilingual Education and Bilingualism, 23*(7), 833–837. doi:10.1080/13670050.2020.1783638

Evans, B. A., & Hornberger, N. H. (2005). No child left behind: Repealing and unpeeling federal language education policy in the United States. *Language Policy, 4*(1), 87–106. https://doi.org/10.1007/s10993-004-6566-2

Faingold, E. D. (2012). Official English in the constitutions and statutes of the fifty states in the United States. *Language Problems and Language Planning, 36*(2), 136–148.

Flores, N., & Chaparro, S. (2017). What counts as language education policy? Developing a materialist anti-racist approach to language activism. *Language Policy, 17*(3), 365–384. doi:10.1007/s10993-017-9433-7

Gándara, P., & Escamilla, K. (2017). Bilingual education in the United States. In O. García, A. Lin, & S. May (Eds.), *Bilingual and multilingual education. Encyclopedia of language and education* (3rd ed.). Springer. https://doi.org/10.1007/978-3-319-02258-1_33

Gándara, P., Losen, D., August, D., Uriarte, M., Gómez, M. C., & Hopkins, M. (2010). Forbidden language: A brief history of U.S. language policy. In P. Gándara & M. Hopkins (Eds.), *Forbidden language: English learners and restrictive language policies* (pp. 20–33). New York: Teachers College Press.

Goldenberg, C., & Wagner, K. (2015). Bilingual education: Revising an American tradition. *American Educator, 39*(3).

Houvouras, S. K. (2001). The effects of demographic variables, ethnic prejudice, and attitudes toward immigration on opposition to bilingual education. *Hispanic Journal of Behavioral Sciences, 23*(2), 136–152.

Imhoff, G. (1990). The position of U.S. English on bilingual education. *The Annals of the American Academy of Political and Social Science, 508*, 48–61.

Jackman, M. R., & Muha, M. J. (1984). Education and intergroup attitudes: Moral enlightenment, superficial democratic commitment, or ideological refinement? *American Sociological Review, 49*, 751–769.

Kim, Y. K., Hutchison, L. A., & Winsler, A. (2015). Bilingual education in the United States: An historical overview and examination of two-way immersion. *Educational Review, 67*(2), 236–252. http://x.doi.org/10.1080/00131911.2013.865593

Kloss, H. (1977). *The American bilingual tradition.* Newberry House Publishers.

Kloss, H. (1998). *The American bilingual tradition. Language in education: Theory and practice No. 88.* Delta Systems Co., Inc.

Kober, N. (2020). *History and evolution of public education in the U.S.* Center for Education Policy.

Latin American Network Information Center. (n.d.). *Country directory.* Retrieved January 11, 2022, from http://lanic.utexas.edu/subject/countries

Lau v. Nichols. 414 U.S. 563 (1974).

Meyer v Nebraska. 262 U.S. 390 (1923).

Migration Policy Institute. (2013). *Timeline: Major U.S. immigration laws 1790–present.* Author. https://www.migrationpolicy.org/sites/default/files/publications/CIR-1790Timeline.pdf

Nieto, D. (2009). A brief history of bilingual education in the United States. *Perspectives on Urban Education, 6*(1), 61–72.

Nieto, S., & Bode, P. (2018). *Affirming diversity: The sociopolitical context of multicultural education.* Pearson.

Ovando, C. J. (2003). Bilingual education in the United States: Historical development and current issues. *Bilingual Research Journal, 27*(1), 1–24. https://doi.org/10.1080/15235882.2003.10162589

Pavlenko, A. (2002). "We have room for but one language here": Language and national identity in the U.S. at the turn of the 20th century. *Multilingua, 21*, 163–196.

Schildkrau, D. J. (2001). Official English and the states: Influences on declaring English the official language in the United States. *Political Research Quarterly, 54*(2), 445–457.

Sinclair, J. (2018). "Starving and suffocating": Evaluation policies and practices during the first 10 years of the U.S. Bilingual Education Act. *International Journal of Bilingual Education and Bilingualism, 21*(6), 710–728. doi:10.1080/13670050.2016.1210565

Spolsky, B. (2004). *Language policy*. Cambridge University Press.

Spring, J. (2001). *The American School 1642–2000* (5th ed.). McGraw-Hill.

Spring, J. (2011). *The American School: A global context from the Puritans to the Obama era* (8th ed.). McGraw-Hill.

Tollefson, J. W. (2002). "The language debates: Preparing for the war in Yugoslavia." *International Journal of the Sociology of Language* 154, 65–82.

Tyack, D., & Cuban, L. (1995). *Tinkering toward Utopia: A century of public school reform*. Harvard University Press.

White, P. R., Mammone, G., & Caldwell, D. (2015). Linguistically based inequality, multilingual education and genre-based literacy development pedagogy: Insights from the Australian experience. *Language and Education, 29*(3), 256–271.

Wiley, T. G. (2007). Accessing language rights in education: A brief history of the US context. *Bilingual Education and Bilingualism, 61*, 89.

Wolgin, P. E. (2015, October 16). *The Immigration and Nationality Act of 1965 turns 50*. Center for American Progress. https://www.americanprogress.org/issues/immigration/news/2015/10/16/123477/the-immigration-and-nationality-act-of-1965-turns-50

Chapter 16

Real Teachers Teaching Real Students

Where Theory Meets Practice— Learning English in Secondary Schools

Glori Hodge Smith

Learning English while simultaneously learning the higher-level and abstract concepts required in secondary school is difficult. There are stories of English Learners (ELs) successfully moving on to college or the workforce, but there are also stories of students giving up and dropping out. It is not always clear what makes the difference. What are effective teachers doing, and what do their practices look like? Are successful teachers engaging in critical pedagogy or culturally relevant teaching practices? Have they developed caring, empathetic relationships with students that result in greater engagement and academic success?

 The following examples of effective teachers illuminate key practices and underlying attitudes that other teachers can emulate as they strive to reach and teach ELs. Though all of them teach ELs, only two teach classes designated as English language development (ELD) or English as a Second Language (ESL) courses; the others have ELs within their mainstream classes. Most of their students are Spanish speakers, and several of the teachers speak Spanish, but two do not.

CAITLYN MICHAELS FERNANDEZ

Caitlyn Michaels Fernandez is a young White woman who teaches both honors-level English language arts and ESL. To make connections and build community with her ELs, most of whom are Latinx, she spends the first several class periods in "getting to know you" activities, and she makes sure students also get to know her. Before the first class ends, they know her husband is a Mexican national and her family speaks Spanish at home.

Invariably, they also find out that Ms. Fernandez will use Spanish in class as needed, to get attention or to explain a concept. Fernandez sets an atmosphere of academic urgency and high expectations for her ELs, but somehow manages to also keep her classroom relaxed and friendly. She follows the adage, "Know your content inside and out, so you can focus on the kids."

In the ESL class, students are organized in groups based on reading level, and are expected to work with partners from the assigned group, though sometimes they can choose to work alone. They are allowed to leave their desks, and even the room, if they prefer another space for working. However, a clear agenda of academic work is present. For example, when a student asks Ms. Fernandez if he can go get a drink, she will ask if he has completed his assignment; if he simply holds up his paper in response to the question, Ms. Fernandez requires him to verbalize "yes" in English.

Ms. Fernandez knows it is important to teach language-minority students the same content as native English-speaking students. Fernandez applies this idea as she regularly teaches the same content to her ELs as to her honors English students, adding scaffolding to support the ELs and adjusting the focus on the skills that are necessary for each student's progress. For example, when teaching essay writing, she uses a graphic organizer on the white board that shows the various parts of an essay.

Students have their own copy and fill it in as the teacher instructs the class using specific examples that address their strengths and weaknesses as seen in previous work. As she teaches the ELs, she will occasionally use Spanish to clarify points or answer questions; by the end of the 45-minute lesson, the students in both courses have filled in their own charts and are beginning to write independently.

As ELs progress and are ready for mainstream English, Fernandez sometimes arranges their schedules so that they move directly into her honors English class. This is done for a variety of reasons. Sometimes, because she knows her students' abilities well, she determines that they are capable of high-level work; at other times she wants to keep struggling students close, where she can quickly see problems and scaffold her instruction for optimal learning. It is not unusual to discover several students in the honors class were once in her ESL class.

MIKE HARTVIG

Mike Hartvig, a middle-aged, monolingual, White man, teaches boys' physical education (P.E.) and is an example of intentional planning to reach all students. When transferred to a school with a much higher Latinx population than where he had previously taught, Hartvig made a list of new skills he needed to acquire. The list included items such as "speak and honor" Spanish, pronounce names correctly, and include Latinx-centric music on the playlist in the weight room. Hartvig studied the sounds of the Spanish alphabet and worked on correct name pronunciation, and he learned basic greetings and a few phrases that would be useful in class.

Coach Hartvig posts important announcements and learning targets on a bulletin board in the hallway between the locker room and the gym. The boys find their names listed on preassigned teams, saving class time and preventing the problems associated with adolescents choosing teammates. Also posted are "Coach Hartvig's ABCs for Success," his guide for discussing important life lessons with his students:

- Avoid negative people, places, and things.
- Believe in yourself.
- Consider the other perspective, and so forth.

As might be expected, P.E. class is usually an energetic frenzy of physical activity, but Coach Hartvig ends class with a short debriefing activity that includes a life lesson. With just 45 minutes for class, Hartvig must plan carefully to fit this in. Sometimes these pep talks are in conjunction with his "ABCs," and other times he might use a successful Latino to illustrate a story of accomplishment. Hartvig does not name or challenge racism in these lessons, but he shows, by example, how to treat all people with respect. Students can see the respect that he gives everyone, greatly diminishing the rivalry and conflicts that can be common in sports activities with adolescent boys.

When meeting parents, Hartvig will often use a bit of Spanish. He feels that his willingness to try to communicate, and to laugh at his own mistakes, allows them to try out their imperfect English. Parents and teacher smile and laugh together, appreciating the difficulties of learning a second language. It does not often eliminate the need for an interpreter at parent-teacher conferences, but it does break the ice and build relationships. His empathy for students and parents learning a new language is real, born of his own attempts to add Spanish to his list of skills. His cultural knowledge and competence are the result of purposeful study.

ROBERT ABBOTT

Robert Abbott, another middle-aged White man, teaches Spanish, a language he learned as a young adult serving a religious mission in Uruguay. His classroom and his practices send the message that Latinx culture and the Spanish language, including its many dialects, are of value.

- The visual curriculum sends a subtle, but clear, anti-racist message. The calendar and every single map, Spanish grammar poster, and inspiring quote on his classroom walls are in Spanish.
- Abbott teaches a heritage Spanish class and, though most of the students are of Mexican descent, he makes sure that different dialects of the language are recognized and looks for opportunities to let students share their familial knowledge. When teaching vocabulary, he will check with one or two students from different countries to see if they have a different word for a particular term. When a classroom video is showing a store in Mexico, he might pause and say, "Sarita, is that similar to the Bolivian experience?" He then draws the student into an instructional conversation where she is the expert in the classroom. He is conscientious about recognizing and honoring language differences and student individuality.
- Abbott intentionally looks for stereotyping that may arise in or outside of class. He helps the students learn to recognize and challenge biases in student interactions, popular culture, and even the texts and instructional films that might be shown in class.

The comfortable, empathetic relationships that can be observed in Abbott's classroom are boosted by his volunteer duties of lunchroom and bus-loading supervision, when he gets to know students in a casual atmosphere. Mr. Abbott believes these activities increase enrollment in his Spanish classes and definitely increase attendance at his advisory period, a time when students are free to go to any classroom or teacher for help with assignments. Many of the students attending advisory are Latinx, some ELs, and it is likely that the Spanish-language wall décor, mentioned above, increases the perception that this is a place where they are welcome.

GERALDO TORRES

Geraldo Torres is a young choral music teacher with high expectations for student achievement. He refers to himself as Hispanic, did not become fluent in Spanish until adulthood, and does not find it necessary to overtly assist his Latinx students. However, there are several specific practices that help his English learners in particular:

- The nature of choral music classes is distinctive from that of other content areas. Students are generally responding "in chorus" to instruction from the teacher. This is an excellent way for language students to improve their pronunciation and intonation of the target language in a comfortable, nonthreatening atmosphere. Because students are singing together and getting group instruction from the teacher, no one feels singled out for correction, and English learners get a lot of practice reading and singing the same words, over and over again.
- Songs from the traditional European canon often have Latin lyrics, and this is an opportunity to let students whose L_1 is any Latin-based language, shine. In Torres's class, they are called into service to help translate and to demonstrate correct pronunciation. Neither the translation nor pronunciation is straightforward, but the student interpreters work it out together. They model pronunciation, correcting and encouraging the others when the pronunciation is difficult. Mr. Torres takes part in the discussion, but sometimes he also needs help: "If I say it wrong (because Spanish is my second language, not my first), [a student might say], 'No, Mr. Torres, it's this way.'" Torres finds such activities to be a positive experience for all.
- Torres understands that for some students his presence is a supportive factor, and he occasionally uses cultural references, jokes, stories, and his ability in Spanish to make connections with his Latinx students. His classroom door is always open for chatting, eating lunch, singing or playing the piano, and sometimes for crying:

> I'll have kids come in here and talk to me and I'm not their choir teacher any more.... It's not about music.... For me to know that sometimes kids feel safe enough to come talk to me about things.... That's gratifying, that they feel safe in here.... Sometimes there is something more important than the classroom.

However, Mr. Torres said those moments are rare. Doing well in school is important, and he expects students to work diligently. They learn quickly that he is "willing to have hard conversations," reprimanding them for doing less than they are capable of.

I don't accept excuses for not putting in the work needed to succeed. When it's necessary, I will tell them stories of living on rice and beans, and of working more than 50 hours a week while taking over 20 credits in college.

He believes students are willing to do hard things if they know he understands their situation and that he cares.

GWEN MACKEY FRASER

Gwen Mackey Fraser is a middle-aged, monolingual White woman, who knows that when ELs are reading, writing, speaking, and listening in English, almost any topic will help improve proficiency. She finds this very freeing as she develops lessons, but chooses carefully, making sure students are learning important information. She often uses the news as lesson material. Helping newcomers make sense of current world events or the culture of their new home is important.

Even school announcements are valuable—ELs often miss important information because announcements from the public address system can be difficult to understand. She also has students do oral presentations for the class on their hometown or compare cultural aspects of the United States and their native country.

Fraser had been teaching ESL for nearly 15 years when she did an action research project on blogging with her intermediate level ESL class. The students created personal weblogs (blogs) and reported their reading and completed other assignments online, rather than with paper and pencil. Fraser had never blogged herself and struggled with teaching the technology skills to the students but thought that understanding and having the skills to use multimedia formats were important in fighting the digital divide and preparing her high school students for their futures (Becker, 2000; Lee, 2006).

She also hoped that the public accessibility of internet blogging would promote more attention to English acquisition. This turned out to be true. The students wrote, on average, 68% more on their blogs than in their composition notebooks and they reported increased attention to detail as a result of the very public nature of their work (Smith, 2009, pp. 66–68). This coincides with the motivational increase when using the internet found by Lam (2000) and Gedera (2011).

Fraser also teaches United States history and government classes where students are a mix of native English speakers and ELs. To help her newcomer students make a connection with the curriculum, she might ask them to compare and contrast similar events from one country to another. Many nations have experienced revolutions and civil wars; when explaining similarities and differences between such events and those in the United States, students can practice their English skills as they write about something they already know and grasp the content of U.S. history.

When learning world events from the U.S. perspective, newcomer students can practice their English skills as they share what they (or their parents) learned about that same event as students in their home country. For example, Fraser's entire class was fascinated as students from Mexico presented on how the Mexican American War of 1846–1848 was taught from the other side of the border.

In addition to teaching ESL and history, Fraser was the school coordinator for English language development for over 20 years. She believes schools and teachers should never deny ELs the curriculum that they deem is important for others (Smith, 2009, pp. 18–19). She often gave suggestions to other teachers that came to her for advice on helping the ELs access their curriculum and succeed on assessments.

- Visual aids are essential: simple stick drawings, maps, photos, videos, Venn diagrams, and other graphic organizers. Similarly, gestures and body language are helpful.
- Simplify whenever possible. Eliminate any items in written work assignments that are not essential.
- Surprisingly, English learners can often explain what they know in a paragraph better than they can complete objective assessments like fill-in-the-blank or multiple choice. This is increased if you encourage them to write what they can in English but allow them to add information in their L_1.
- Do not dock points for their English grammar or spelling in a content-area assignment. Read between the errors and search for what they are trying to express.
- If possible, point out cognates and near-cognates between languages.
- Encourage students to find the content online or in texts in their native language and use the information to help them bridge between their knowledge and their English proficiency. Similarly, allow the use of L_1 between students—this is background knowledge and can help them make connections.
- Smile often and be encouraging—try not to share how challenging it is to find yourself helping with English acquisition when you were trained to teach biology, history, and so on. This last suggestion comes from ELs who shared their experiences with Fraser, sometimes participating in professional development presentations. They often stressed the difference it made if the teacher was friendly and believed in their ability to succeed.

The teachers introduced in this chapter are not particularly well-versed in the ideas of culturally relevant pedagogy (CRP) or critical race theory (CRT), but they all care deeply about their students and spend time thinking about the best ways to make connections and teach the curriculum. They thoughtfully engage in practices that resonate with those pedagogical approaches.

Culturally relevant pedagogy is derived from critical race theory (Ladson-Billings, 1994, 1995), so naturally the teaching practices of both overlap in many ways. Both Ladson-Billings and Brown-Jeffy and Cooper (2011) delineated themes of CRP, and the teachers profiled here address these concepts.

- Identity: Abbott and Hartvig explicitly speak of cultural backgrounds with respect, supporting the maintenance of students' home cultures. Deferring to the knowledge that students already have, they recognize the funds of knowledge (Gonzalez et al., 2005) that they bring to school, and Fraser is tapping into this knowledge when she has students share and compare transnational knowledge. With an understanding born of his life experiences, Mr. Torres makes cultural connections with his Latinx students and helps them to bridge between their home environment, family values, and the mainstream culture of the school. Neither Abbott, Hartvig, Torres, nor Fraser are guilty of practicing subtractive education (Valenzuela, 1999), which ignores or devalues the culture or learning that takes place at home. Similarly, Fernandez recognizes that lack of English proficiency does not indicate lack of intelligence (Solórzano, 1997).
- Equity and excellence: Fernandez has high expectations of academic proficiency for her students and provides an excellent example of teaching for equity as she offers ELs the same curriculum as honors students. Ladson-Billings (1995) suggested that teachers should guide students to recognize injustice and take steps to rectify it, empowering them to be a force for societal change. Of the teachers highlighted in this chapter, only Abbott, with his attention to stereotyping, explicitly addresses this anti-racist pedagogy. But academic achievement is crucial to that next step; if students do not learn the academic skills of the powerful majority, they cannot hope to compete nor be in a position to change society.
- Developmental appropriateness: Recognizing that not all students are at the same developmental levels is important, but is sometimes used as an excuse to water down the curriculum for ELs. Fernandez recognizes that students are at a developmental level in which they are capable of understanding argumentation and that being limited in English proficiency does not limit their ability to think critically. Mr. Torres exemplifies high expectations when he introduces an all-Latin piece of music to middle school students. Teaching the connection between Spanish and Latin is

knowledge that many adolescents do not have and has the added benefit of elevating the status of Spanish.
- Teaching the whole child: Hartvig finds time to teach about life, not just exercise and sports; Fraser's lessons help students understand their new home, not just focus on English vocabulary and grammar; Abbott works to fight stereotyping, not just teach the Spanish language; Torres and Abbott both find time and space to talk and listen to students outside of curricular matters.
- Student-teacher relationships: When the teacher and students are not of the same ethnic or cultural background, extra communication is needed to develop commonalities and build empathetic relationships. Hartvig's intentional actions help him to build authentically empathetic relationships with the Latinos in his classes. Just as Milner (2011) found, the students need to get to know the teacher in order to develop trusting relationships. Abbott, Fraser, and Fernandez all plan for lessons and time to get to know students. Only Torres is from a similar background to most of the ELs in his classroom and he made time to share that information with students. Accepting the students' expertise and allowing his errors to be corrected is very gracious. This is a respectful and effective way to publicly acknowledge student skills and abilities.

Empathy is the unifying factor that all these teachers share, and this leads to student success. Empathetic teachers "take on the perspective of another culture" (McAllister & Irvine, 2002, p. 433), and establishing and maintaining empathetic relationships is what teaching requires. Communicating genuine care and empathy for students often results in student willingness to engage with the curriculum and achieve academically (Milner, 2010; Saunders, 2012; Seltzer-Kelly, 2009; Warren, 2012). Milner (2007) explained that many teachers say they care, but it is their caring words and actions that actually make a difference.

Teachers of different personalities, dispositions, and skills are able to communicate the care and concern that they have for students, to build empathetic relationships that inspire students to be more engaged with their learning and achieve.

REFERENCES

Becker, H. J. (2000). Who's wired and who's not: Children's access to and use of computer technology. *The Future of Children, 10*(2), 44–75.

Brown-Jeffy, S., & Cooper, J. E. (2011). Toward a conceptual framework of culturally relevant pedagogy: An overview of the conceptual and theoretical literature. *Teacher Education Quarterly, 38*(1), 65–84.

Gedera, D. S. P. (2011). Integration of weblogs in developing language skills of ESL learners. *International Journal of Technology in Teaching and Learning, 7*(2), 124–135.

Gonzalez, N., Moll, L. C., & Amanti, C. (2005). *Funds of knowledge: Theorizing practices in households, communities, and classrooms.* Lawrence Erlbaum and Associates, Inc.

Ladson-Billings, G. (1994). *The dreamkeepers: Successful teachers of African American children.* Jossey-Bass.

Ladson-Billings, G. (1995). But that's just good teaching! The case for culturally relevant pedagogy. *Theory Into Practice, 34*(2), 159–165. doi:10.1080/00405849509543675

Lam, W. S. E. (2000). L$_2$ literacy and the design of the self: A case study of a teenager writing on the internet. *TESOL Quarterly, 34*(3), 445–482.

Lee, R. (2006). The effective learning outcomes of ESL elementary and secondary school students utilizing educational technology infused with constructivist pedagogy. *International Journal of Instructional Media, 33*(1), 87–93.

McAllister, G., & Irvine, J. J. (2002). The role of empathy in teaching culturally diverse students: A qualitative study of teachers' beliefs. *Journal of Teacher Education, 53*(5), 433–443.

Milner, H. R. (2007). African American males in urban schools: No excuses—teach and empower. *Theory Into Practice, 6*(3), 239–246.

Milner, H. R. (2010). *Culture, curriculum, and identity in education.* Palgrave MacMillan.

Milner, H. (2011). Culturally relevant pedagogy in a diverse urban classroom. *Urban Review, 43*(1), 66–89.

Saunders, J. M. (2012). Intersecting realities: A novice's attempts to use critical literacy to access her students' figured worlds. *Multicultural Education, 19*(2), 18–23.

Seltzer-Kelly, D. (2009). Adventures in critical pedagogy: A lesson in U.S. history. *Teacher Education Quarterly, 36*(1), 149–162.

Smith, G. H. (2009). Obtaining, processing, and constructing English: Blogging in the ESL classroom. *Journal of Media Literacy Education.* http://www.jmle.org/index.php/JMLE/article/viewFile/37/8

Solórzano, D. G. (1997). Images and words that wound: Critical race theory, racial stereotyping, and teacher education. *Teacher Education Quarterly, 24,* 5–19. http://dist.lib.usu.edu/login?url=http://search.ebscohost.com/login.aspx?direct=true&db=eue&AN=507592555&site=ehost-live

Valenzuela, A. (1999). *Subtractive schooling: U.S. Mexican youth and the politics of caring.* State University of New York Press.

Warren, C. (2012). *Empathic interaction: White female teachers and their Black male students* [Unpublished doctoral dissertation]. University of Illinois, Chicago.

Chapter 17

Creating Social Change for English Language Learners by Improving Access to Grade-Level Instruction

Charity Funfe Tatah Mentan, Darrell Peterson, Yi-Chen Wu, Kristin Kline Liu, and Kym O'Donnell

There has been a dramatic growth in the number of students who are English Language Learners (ELLs) in U.S. public schools, from 3.8 million in 2000 (8.1%) to 5 million in 2017 (10.1%; National Center for Education Statistics [NCES], 2020).

Due to this rapid growth, there is an urgent need to get educators ready to provide accessible, high-quality, grade-level instruction for ELLs. Doing so will create social change for these students. Successful communication between families (including parents, guardians, and caregivers), educators (including teachers, administrators, and service providers), and students plays a significant role in creating meaningful instruction and assessment for ELLs and improving student outcomes.

Unfortunately, ELLs are often denied the chance to meaningfully participate in grade-level academic content due to the belief they must first be proficient in English. We see the results of this inequity in limited course enrollment in secondary schools, low state assessment scores, high dropout rates, and low graduation rates. In turn, this results in limited post-secondary options and diminished quality of life.

In order to effect the social change necessary to improve educational outcomes for ELLs, educators need to transform how they collaborate. Students, families, and educators can collaborate in a culturally and linguistically responsive manner to provide equitable access to high-quality grade-level instruction to improve student outcomes.

To illustrate how collaboration among educators and families can create social change, you will meet 16-year-old Ji-Yoo, who recently moved to the United States from Korea, has beginning levels of English proficiency, and has strong math skills that he developed in Korean. Ji-Yoo's experiences in math class at his U.S. school will serve as an example as this chapter addresses:

- definitions of the term *ELL,*
- seeing student characteristics as assets,
- how collaboration can help improve students' academic learning opportunities, and
- how to support social change and cultural relevancy through professional development.

DEFINING THE TERM *ELL*

To appropriately serve ELLs, educators, policy makers, and stakeholders need to know who the students are. The term *ELL* is specific to a group of students who are eligible to receive English language development (ELD) services, as described in Every Student Succeeds Act (2015). Eligibility for ELD services is typically determined through home language surveys that establish a language other than English is spoken in the home and through English proficiency screening assessments.

For our example student, Ji-Yoo, the home language survey completed by his family indicated they speak only Korean at home. The screening assessment showed that he had beginning-level skills in English reading, writing, listening, and speaking. Thus, Ji-Yoo qualified for ELD services as a level 1/newcomer. However, staff at Ji-Yoo's school did not initially know much more than these basic facts about him.

SEEING STUDENT CHARACTERISTICS AS ASSETS

Despite the common identification process, ELLs like Ji-Yoo possess a wide variety of characteristics (e.g., cultural backgrounds, multilingualism, prior knowledge, skills) that should be viewed as assets. Understanding these assets is important to providing educational opportunities that will create social change. For example, ELLs are often fluent in one or more languages and have a rich experiential knowledge base, developed within their culture, from which to draw during the learning process. In Ji-Yoo's case, he had earned top marks in pre-calculus classes in Korea and wanted to study math at an American university, but he did not have the English proficiency to express what he already knew.

Ji-Yoo's school counselor, unaware of the assets he brought to learning, used the English proficiency screener results to place Ji-Yoo in a basic skills math class. She felt that the basic math class would allow him to learn key math vocabulary in English. This decision, made solely based on test scores showing what Ji-Yoo did not know, resulted in an opportunity gap for Ji-Yoo. He would not be able to take the advanced math courses at his new high school before he graduated, and this would affect his college plans. His parents immediately asked the school for a meeting to discuss ways Ji-Yoo might be included in the high school pre-calculus class with supports provided to help him be successful. The English language development (ELD) teacher, Ms. Jones, convened the meeting.

As a first step, Ms. Jones gathered resources from the Improving Instruction for English Learners Through Improved Accessibility Decisions (Improving Instruction) project, funded by the Office of English Language Acquisition (Award #T365Z160115). This project supports educators in creating accessible grade-level instruction that builds on ELLs' strengths.

HOW COLLABORATION CAN HELP INCREASE STUDENTS' LEARNING OPPORTUNITIES

Silos in K–12 Schools

As seen in Ji-Yoo's example, many school districts across the country designate responsibility for instructional decision-making for ELLs to ELD specialists. However, these students may be taught in general education classes where general education teachers may have little preparation in simultaneously developing a student's English proficiency and content learning. Academic silos such as these, where different teachers work alone to meet the needs of the same student based on a partial understanding of the student's needs, result in fragmented and ineffective learning experiences for ELLs. It is, for this reason, that collaboration among educators and families is essential to providing culturally relevant education.

Ms. Jones understood that creating meaningful access to pre-calculus for Ji-Yoo would require shared responsibility between Ji-Yoo, his family, his math teacher, and herself, with support from the school principal. Shared responsibility entailed collaborative decision-making about ways to appropriately scaffold his learning in the classroom.

Collaboration

To create equitable instructional environments that appropriately support the achievement of ELLs, every teacher, not just the ELD specialist, needs to know the whole student (Noddings, 2005) and plan learning opportunities based on that knowledge. The interconnected tenets of culturally relevant pedagogy (CRP) (Ladson-Billings, 2014) help teams explore how they might use the knowledge gained to create cultural relevancy for English learners in the classroom by

- prioritizing students' learning needs,
- embedding students' home cultures authentically into the learning, and
- validating students' ways of knowing instead of focusing on their perceived limitations in the classroom.

Ladson-Billings (2014) advocated for culturally sustaining pedagogy, an approach that includes the critical component of cultural relevancy, to enhance equitable access to high-quality educational outcomes.

Collaboration Between Educators and Families

Engaging families in decision-making gives them a voice in the academic progress of their child, but their involvement must be meaningful. In Ji-Yoo's case, Ms. Jones invited Ji-Yoo, his parents, a Korean language interpreter, the counselor, and the math teacher for a collaborative conversation. Prior to that meeting, Ms. Jones ensured that everyone had the background and understanding needed to be equal partners in the conversation. She shared with the team a series of practical tools, called the Parent-Educator Toolkit (see https://nceo.info/about/projects/improving-instruction/parent-educator-toolkit).

Components of the toolkit described successful two-way communication between school staff and families of ELLs, the use of a language interpreter, and common supports ("accessibility features") for ELLs in grade-level general education classrooms. There are separate materials designed for parents, educators, and school principals. The language interpreter reviewed the materials with Ji-Yoo's parents in Korean.

At the collaborative conversation, Ms. Jones and the math teacher presented a list of ways to design calculus instruction so that all students, including Ji-Yoo, had multiple ways to receive information and respond. This concept is referred to as Universal Design for Learning (UDL; for more information, see https://udlguidelines.cast.org). For example, the math teacher could allow students to choose how they would complete math problems:

writing out answers on paper, typing responses on a computer, playing a math game, or choosing the correct solution from a set of multiple-choice options.

In addition, Ji-Yoo's math teacher planned to collaborate with Ms. Jones to incorporate whole-class language-development strategies into the math classroom. For example, one technique is shared partner dialogues emphasizing oral use of new math vocabulary before students are required to read and write that vocabulary in a lesson. Again, these strategies benefit all students, including Ji-Yoo, and contribute to more equitable outcomes for ELLs.

Ms. Jones explained that after embedding access strategies for all students into the instructional plan, Ji-Yoo could receive individualized supports that he needed to be successful (e.g., placing him in class with a bilingual Korean-English speaking student so he could ask questions in his strongest language, selectively using a Korean-English electronic dictionary, simplifying the language on assignments and tests, etc.). These supports would help create meaningful access to the course content as well as to math assessments.

As Ms. Jones described the options available and explained how they would work, she invited Ji-Yoo and his parents to ask questions and to recommend the supports that would work best, given what they knew about Ji-Yoo. Their shared knowledge was documented in an electronic accessibility plan that all the meeting attendees, as well as the school principal, could access and revise through continued discussion throughout the year (for a possible template of a plan, see https://nceo.umn.edu/docs/OnlinePubs/II_EL_accessibility_form.docx).

Collaboration Among Educators

There are four different capacities in which educator collaboration is vital to providing meaningful access to instruction: individualized accessibility decisions, co-teaching, and administrative supports. Examples of each type of collaboration follow.

Individualized Accessibility Decisions

Educators as agents of social change should collaborate with other teachers as they develop lessons to ensure ELLs have access to the language and academic content all students are expected to learn (Lindahl & Baecher, 2019). One collaboration strategy, as previously mentioned, involves educators working together with the student and family to complete an English Learner Accessibility Plan for individual ELLs.

Teachers should continue to meet on a regular basis to exchange information about students and monitor the effectiveness of accessibility plans. For example, an ELD specialist and a high school history teacher may meet to discuss the experience of ELLs in a U.S. history class. The ELD specialist can share and explain relevant English proficiency data and provide suggestions regarding how instruction might be adapted to support the students' differing English proficiency growth. The U.S. history teacher might ask for feedback on how an upcoming test could be made more accessible for the ELLs and what specific supports could be provided to individual students so they can demonstrate what they know and can do.

Co-Teaching

Effective collaboration can also come through co-teaching, with both academic and ELD teachers working together to teach the same class at the same time. Co-teachers plan, teach, assess, and reflect together. This takes dedicated time to be successful, but it is an extremely effective way to improve ELLs' learning outcomes. Through collaboration, the roles of the ELD specialist and general education teachers begin to meld and create space for sharing of expertise and joint problem solving that generates multiple solutions (Risko & Bromley, 2001). In this shared space, departments function better to meet students' needs (Theoharis & O'Toole, 2011).

Administrative Supports

Effective collaboration cannot occur without the support of school administrators, particularly school principals. It is important for administrators to provide the logistics necessary for collaborative planning, teaching, and reflecting, as well as ongoing, relevant professional learning. Among the many effective ways for an administrator to support collaboration is the use of professional learning communities (PLCs) as the collaborative norm. In addition, administrative staff should make sure that co-teaching is supported both instructionally and logistically (Honigsfeld & Dove, 2010).

HOW TO ENCOURAGE SOCIAL CHANGE AND CULTURAL RELEVANCY THROUGH PROFESSIONAL DEVELOPMENT

To ensure that the educational system is contributing to social change, it is imperative that educators are well trained and well prepared. Ji-Yoo's math teacher and counselor had attended a few one-time workshops, e-learning modules, and conferences on working with ELLs. During the collaborative conversation, it became clear that a more comprehensive professional development approach was needed for all school staff to serve ELLs equitably and positively affect student achievement (see Reed, 2000).

The principal knew that professional development should consist of sustained, intensive activities grounded in deepening teachers' knowledge of content as well as including issues of culture, language, race, and collaboration (Theoharis & O'Toole, 2011). He also understood that educators needed opportunities to practice what they learned and to reflect on the results of incorporating their learning into instruction. Paris (2012) recommended teachers do all of this while ensuring that their practice remains aligned with standards and the principles of equity in culturally sustaining pedagogy.

The Improving Instruction project created one approach to improving teacher professional development, based on a variety of coordinated opportunities (see https://nceo.info/about/projects/improving-instruction/home). It provides online instruction through two e-learning modules, which can be completed any time and any place (asynchronously). The modules focus on methods for providing ELLs with universally designed, accessible instruction and assessment. The modules also provide tools and resources to support teacher learning including a literature review, presentations for a deeper dive into specific issues, and templates for forms like the English Learner Accessibility Plan.

One approach to providing a deeper dive is to schedule follow-up webinars for teachers to come together (virtually) to share ideas and experiences of working collaboratively to make content more accessible for ELLs, as well as reflect on their practice. Used along with the Parent-Educator Toolkit, these components create a systemic approach to professional development that incorporates learning, practice, and reflection. The systemic approach incorporates students, families, and administrators as collaborators in the decision-making process to better meet the needs of ELLs and improve their outcomes.

This chapter shed light on the increasing population of ELLs and the need to understand their individual characteristics and assets. It also illustrated the need for implementing principles of social change and culturally relevant pedagogy. A set of practical tools for making collaborative decisions about accessible instruction and assessment for ELLs was shared, including online professional development modules with an accompanying discussion guide.

Teams can use the English learner accessibility plan template to coordinate and document the specific accessibility supports that best meet an individual student's needs and use the Parent-Educator Toolkit to create and sustain collaborative partnerships between educators and parents, as well as school principals. When these tools are used in a collaborative environment that includes all stakeholders, a foundation is laid for social change in formal (school) and informal (community-based organization) settings serving ELLs and their families.

REFERENCES

Every Student Succeeds Act (ESSA), Public Law 114–95, U.S. Statutes at Large 129 (2015): 1802.

Honigsfeld, A., & Dove, M. G. (2010). *Collaboration and co-teaching: Strategies for English learners*. Corwin Press.

Ladson-Billings, G. (2014). Culturally relevant pedagogy 2.0: Aka the remix. *Harvard Educational Review, 84*(1), 74–84.

Lindahl, K., & Baecher, L. (2019). Preparing TESOL specialists for K–12 contexts. In L. C. de Oliveira (Ed.), *The handbook of TESOL in K–12* (pp. 357–369). Wiley.

National Center for Education Statistics. (2020). *The condition of education—English Language Learners in public schools*. https://nces.ed.gov/programs/coe/indicator_cgf.asp

Noddings, N. (2005). What does it mean to educate the whole child? *Educational Leadership, 63*(1), 8.

Paris, D. (2012). Culturally sustaining pedagogy: A needed change in stance, terminology, and practice. *Educational Researcher, 41*(3), 93–97.

Reed, J. (2000). The importance of professional development for teachers. *Educational Horizons, 78*(3), 117–118.

Risko, V. J., & Bromley, K. D. (2001). New visions of collaboration. In V. J. Risko & K. D. Bromley (Eds.), *Collaboration for diverse learners: Viewpoints and practices* (pp. 9–19). Routledge.

Theoharis, G., & O'Toole, J. (2011). Leading inclusive ELL: Social justice leadership for English language learners. *Educational Administration Quarterly, 47*(4), 646–688. https://doi.org/10.1177/0013161X11401616

Chapter 18

Binds and Unravels
Science Teachers Deepening Learning for English Language Learners

Analis Carattini-Ruiz

In the last 50 years, the United States has experienced an upsurge of K–12 students whose native language(s) is a language other than English, often referred to as English Language Learners and more recently as multilingual learners (MLs).[1] MLs in U.S. schools come from a myriad of cultural and linguistic backgrounds, educational experiences, and socioeconomic statuses. This influx has changed school demographics nationwide, creating a sense of urgency to correspondingly shift traditional educational practices toward more equitable practices.

A popular strategy offered by districts nationwide to alleviate the many issues with traditional professional development methods is to replace them with ongoing job-embedded professional learning communities (PLCs).[2] Unfortunately, the myriad conceptualizations of PLCs make their implementation difficult.

In this chapter, five middle school science teachers embarked on a journey and shared their experiences as they participated in a 1-year study to transform their district-adopted PLC into an equity-based PLC in support of MLs. Drawing from whiteness theories, this study explores how discourses of whiteness that are ubiquitous to the U.S. school system are limiting the education of MLs. Specifically, this study inquired deeply into the following questions:

1. How did discourses of whiteness, which are institutionalized in school districts' policies and systems, create institutional binds[3] that shaped science teachers' district professional learning community (PLC)?
2. How did science teachers' engagement in a co-created equity-driven PLC unravel[4] their individual binds and guide them toward rethinking their pedagogical practices with ELLs?
3. How did science teachers' pedagogical practices for and about ELLs actually shift following engagement with this equity-driven PLC?

SCIENCE CONTENT PLCS AT ELLEN OCHOA MIDDLE SCHOOL

Ellen Ochoa Middle School in Las Colinas School District[5] is one of the most diverse middle schools with an ML population of 141 students of a student population of 1,031 students, comprising 16% of the whole student body. In the area of science, which was the focus for this study, MLs scored 5.6% and their White counterparts 38%. That is a 32.4% gap in science content achievement performance between MLs and their White counterparts based on a 100% proficiency metric. These achievement performance scores illustrate the never-ceasing gap created by an educational system that has yet to figure out how to engage MLs pedagogically.

Walking through the hallways of Ellen Ochoa Middle School, one can notice the diverse student population who attend there. The walls display norms for behaviors, posters to remind students of the deep learning competencies of *critical thinking, collaboration, communication, creativity, character*, and *citizenship* (6Cs), as well as student work and messages representing diversity. On the surface, the learning environment there appears to be inclusive; however, what about the pedagogical practices employed by teachers of MLs?

The science teachers at this school come from various educational backgrounds and years of teaching experience. The Ellen Ochoa Middle School has five science teachers. Currently, three of the five teachers teach seventh grade. Some of them also teach eighth and ninth grade. It is a small department serving the academic needs of over 900 students. There are large size classes for each of these teachers' classrooms. Ellen Ochoa Middle School's science team comes from various backgrounds, languages, experiences, and reasons for coming to the profession of teaching science. These characteristics, experiences, and backgrounds play a significant role in coming together as a team, their ways of thinking, talking, making sense, enacting, and ultimately reflecting on their pedagogical practices for teaching science to MLs. For example, Alex and Roland have over 30 years of teaching experience and over 25 years at this school. Whereas Ania, William, and Jacob are within their first three years of experience, this school is their first teaching assignment. In addition, Ania is the only person of color in the team coming from a Pacific Islander background.

As a team, they have been engaging with the PLC Results Cycle[6] for less than 3 years, for about 1 hour per week to plan instruction and assessments. Las Colinas School District has designed and implemented a districtwide framework called the PLC Results Cycle to guide PLC implementation efforts. The PLC Results Cycle shows how the PLC process is framed to guide school-based teams toward:

1. Identifying the essentials or learning targets, leading teams to design team-level learning goals, and designing assessments and instruction that best align with the learning targets.
2. Delivering Tier I instruction.
3. Administering common assessments to gauge the effectiveness of Tier I instruction.
4. Collecting and analyzing the data from the administered assessments and depending on the outcomes, teams revisiting the learning goals and determine the next steps, and
5. Determining which students need interventions and which students need extensions.
6. Engaging in the collaborative inquiry process where they reflect, discuss ways they can refine their practice, and target areas of improvement before moving into the subsequent PLC Results Cycle unit of study.

The expectation is that this cycle is repeated for every essential standard and planned during weekly teams' PLC meetings. Theoretically, this process should provide teachers with the time and space where they deeply reflect on their pedagogical practices based on collected and analyzed student data.

INSTITUTIONAL BINDS: SCIENCE CONTENT PLC

Discourses of whiteness at the institutional level[7] create institutional *binds* that shape the personal/relational level of science teachers' engagement with PLCs and the pedagogical practices provided to MLs in the science classroom. Let's look at some concrete examples on how discourses of whiteness created institutional *binds* that shaped, first, the structure of the district's PLC; second, the science teachers' engagement with the district's PLC; and third, the pedagogical practices the teachers provided to MLs.

Standardization and Tangible Student Outcomes

The district PLC centered both standardization and tangible student outcomes. Standardization and tangible effects are byproducts of discourses of whiteness at play creating material and tangible effects in ways that advance the academic opportunities for some students—White and native-English-speaking peers—while denying those same opportunities to MLs. Initially, the science team spent the majority of the district's PLC time discussing logistics for standardized tests, finalizing labs, and reviewing assessment questions. Ania, one of the first-year teachers, shared, "I feel like most of PLC we're discussing the evaluation part . . . What I get from it is that we focus on what they got from the test scores" (personal communication, October 3, 2019).

For a first-year teacher, test scores and assessment questions do not necessarily support her professional-development needs. Besides, how to develop content knowledge, academic language, and delivering effective instruction were not common topics discussed as teachers engaged with the PLC Results Cycle.

Conversations Related to MLs Were Limited or Nonexistent

The language regarding student learning in the district's PLC was broad and general. William shared, "I don't know if I can think of a time where on a Monday with the science department we said, 'We are going to do this to benefit language learners'" (personal communication, May 6, 2019).

For the science teachers, conversations regarding multilingual learners in the context of the district's PLCs were rare. MLs' invisibility to the district's PLC conversations represent discourses of evasiveness (Frankenberg, 1993), in an "out of sight, out of mind" disposition. The team members often referred to MLs as either "your" or "those" students and not necessarily as "ours" or "our" students, keeping the team from fully exercising collective responsibility for these students.

Normalization of Tracking Systems

One of the unintended consequences from the district's PLC Results Cycle was tracking students into interventions or extensions; basically, the team only intervened for some students and extended for a few others. This practice perpetuates a status quo in which the system extends and accelerates the learning of some students while tracking other students, usually MLs, into a Tier II system[8] set by lower expectations. Thus, this creates artificial barriers for the haves and have-nots, all in the name of student learning.

Consequently, this tracks MLs into interventions without providing them adequate Tier I[9] instruction and denying them deep learning opportunities. Patel (2016) argued, "The privileged need no intervention; they have already achieved" (p. 24). This scenario continues to perpetuate a divide between MLs and students of color and their White, native-English-speaking students, thus continuing to maintain the status quo and its power so that teachers have no need to problematize their pedagogical practices as long as they are justified by placing the blame on MLs for their academic underachievement.

INDIVIDUAL SCIENCE TEACHERS' BINDS

Relatedly, the institutional binds and the teachers' individual binds were inextricably linked. Science teachers displayed individual binds as followed:

1. They did not associate PLCs as the space to develop professionally.
2. They felt ill-equipped to teach MLs.
3. They embodied a deficit disposition toward MLs.
4. They oversimplified science content for MLs.
5. They held low expectations toward MLs.

One example that demonstrated multiple individual binds was shared by Roland in this way:

> The current challenges, like always, is our population. It seems to be increasing in language, ESL, or what I call ESL home speakers. I'd say it's a large part of the population, so we're still being challenged with trying to outline that and have everyone understand what we're doing for *those* ESL students. . . . The ESL doesn't mean anything to me. And so really, it's just . . . it's not so much the ESL students, every once in a while, there's language that we talked about and say, "Well, they're not getting this." "They're not getting this because this language." But often it's *just the ability* within that population. (personal communication, May 6, 2019, emphasis added)

To Roland, learning English as a new language was a barrier to MLs' education. This leads to an underlying assumption that MLs' abilities to learn are limited; as he states, "It's just the ability within that population."

Unfortunately, it is common among educators in K–12 education to perceive MLs as broken rather than whole, or see learning English as a new language as a barrier rather than an asset for learning two languages and becoming bilingual. Alim and Paris (2017) cautioned educators to "see the outcome of learning as additive rather than subtractive, as remaining whole rather than framed as broken, as critical strengths rather than replacing deficits" (p. 1). Learning English as a new language is part of MLs' identity and as such should be developed to its full potential.

SCIENCE TEACHERS' PLC UNRAVELS: THE JOURNEY

The *binds*, as shared above, made visible the ways science education is denied to MLs. Yet the science teachers were able to engage in the co-creation of an equity-driven PLC as a way to *unravel* the *binds* created at the individual teacher level in order to shift their pedagogical practices for and about MLs. Although all institutional *binds* remained unchanged, the individual science teachers' *binds* were *unraveled* by varying degrees. Let's take a look at how the science teachers unraveled their individual binds.

Layering Existing District's Frameworks to Benefit MLs

The science teachers' journey began in the spring in 2018. In the summer, the science teachers decided to engage in a series of professional learning opportunities to explore how to improve their pedagogical practices for and about MLs. At that time, the science teachers became aware of how they were complicit in perpetuating these *binds*. Immediately, they expressed a desire to change their pedagogical practices; however, not all to the same degree.

The science teachers explored and analyzed multiple frameworks, such as the CREDE[10] standards specifically focusing on contextualization and discourses, and the work of Beltran et al. (2013) on the 5Es[11] and the 6Cs.[12] Through this collaborative deep-inquiry learning experience, science teachers built on their background knowledge, and reflected and applied what was central to the education of MLs through layering.[13]

As a result, the teachers discovered a missing element from Beltran et al.'s (2013) work, one additional *E* that they conceptualized as *enhance*. Adding one more *E* to the 5E model led to a change in the model's name to the 5E+[plus].[14] The team began to process how they could best integrate the 6Cs in the context of science teaching. They understood that developing the 6Cs as competencies in students would augment the opportunities for learning at deeper levels. With this in mind, the team layered the 6Cs onto the 5E+[plus]. As a result, the layering process categorized the pedagogical practices as follows:

1. Engage: Critical Thinking
2. Explore: Critical Thinking, and Collaboration
3. Explain: Critical Thinking, Collaboration, and Communication

4. Enhance +: Critical Thinking, Collaboration, Communication, and Creativity
5. Extend: Critical Thinking, Collaboration, Communication, Creativity, Character, and Citizenship
6. Evaluate: Critical Thinking, Collaboration, Communication, Creativity, Character, and Citizenship.

The 5E+[plus] and the 6Cs represent the pedagogical practices that extend Tier I instruction. When enacted as a collaborative inquiry and planning experience, the science teachers can make science education understandable, accessible, and equitable for MLs.

PLC Conversations About MLs

Conversations regarding MLs in PLCs were emerging but limited. Although MLs remained a scarce topic in PLCs, it is important to understand what is playing into the slow movement of the science team toward centering MLs in science education. The district PLC's dominant curriculum of the standards and assessments, traditionally, is what has been centered. Despite the district's strong influence, teachers made some shifts that became visible through teachers' own mirroring[15] process. For example, Alex consistently enacted all 5E+[plus] practices throughout cycles two and three. William shifted from enacting sometimes *Explain* as a practice in cycle two to enacting *Explore, Explain, Enhance, and Extend* at the end of cycle three. Ania shifted from enacting *Explain and Enhance* in cycle two to enacting *Engage, Explore, Explain,* and *Enhance* at the end of cycle three. Jacob shifted from enacting *Engage and Enhance* in cycle two and reverted to enacting *Engage and Explore* at the end of cycle three. Roland remained the same by only enacting *Engage and Explore* in cycle two and at the end of cycle three of this study. It is worth noting that before engaging in this study, most teachers were already enacting the practices of *Engage and Explore*. The practices of *Explain, Enhance+, and Extend* were introduced and developed as part of this study.

A Mirroring Effect

As the science team engaged in a deep learning inquiry experience, they reconceptualized the district's PLC Results Cycle Framework into an equity-driven PLC for science education. Reconceptualizing the district's *PLC Results Cycle* to an equity-driven PLC shifted the collaborative inquiry and planning process as follows:

1. identify the essentials or learning targets leading teams to design team-level learning goals
2. design assessments and instruction that best align with the learning targets
3. deliver Tier I instruction (*Engage and Explore*)
4. deep learning opportunities by extending the learning for all students (*Explain, Enhance +*, and *Extend* for all)
5. administer common assessments to gauge the effectiveness of the Tier I instruction
6. collect and analyze the data from the administered assessments
7. determine as a teacher which students need additional supports teams
8. reflect and engage as teams in the collaborative inquiry process for the next unit of study

At a team level, the main shifts occurred in the planning and delivery of Tier I instruction. By spending additional time delving deeper into the content and concepts through the pedagogical practices of the 5E+[plus] and the 6Cs, MLs outcomes improved, and fewer MLs required interventions. Moreover, through an emerging collaborative inquiry approach of the equity-driven PLC, each teacher displayed in one way or another their own shifts in relation to this process through mirroring. Mirroring, as a reflective and reflexive orientation, is how teachers made decisions in the moment of what they felt comfortable enacting. William described it as follows:

> It's helped me a lot I think because I usually am a man of few words. I don't talk a lot. So usually when I plan things, I don't plan for talking because it's not something that I enjoy but it's such an important part of their learning, especially multilingual learners. So, it's been an interesting change for me, and I like what it's doing for the classroom too. (personal communication, October 3, 2020)

William seemed to internalize the *explain* component the most. His decision to not use *explain* or science talk earlier in the process exemplified discourses of evasiveness pedagogically limiting access and opportunity for MLs and thus reproducing inequitable practices.

Reflecting on the Equity-Driven PLC

Teachers' perceptions of how the equity-driven PLC was translated into their pedagogical practices continue to evolve; however, those practices were not fully integrated into these students' everyday experiences. Moving a team to embody and enact the equity-driven components they co-created is not an easy task; it takes time, ongoing coaching, mentorship, and discussions on continuous improvement of teachers' pedagogical practices for and about MLs in science education in the context of their PLCs.

An unexpected outcome of shifting the science teachers' district PLC to an equity-based PLC was MLs' sudden improvement in end-of-unit assessments after teachers attempted three to four of the equity-based PLC cycle.

MLs' Academic Outcomes > Tier II Interventions

The most impactful shift between the district's PLC Results Cycle and the equity-driven PLC was that the equity-driven PLC required teachers to extend learning for all students through the provision of deep learning experiences as an extension of Tier I instruction. The equity-driven PLC offers the possibility to significantly reduce the number of students taught in Tier II instruction as a result of evaluating the learning too early and surface-type instruction that was inadequate in reaching all students to begin with, especially for MLs.

Alex reported:

> The 7th grade science has had 4 PLC equity-driven cycles so far, biology has had 3 PLC equity-driven cycles. The integration of 5E+[plus] happened in each cycle for both 7th grade and biology and the following 6Cs were integrated in each cycle in these courses: 7th Grade: *collaboration, communication,* and *critical thinking* (*creativity* was also integrated into two of the cycles), biology: *collaboration, communication, creativity,* and *critical thinking.* The *Evaluate* happened after *Extend* for all students in my classroom. I extended for all. (personal communication, November 25, 2019)

Consequently, Alex reported positive student achievement outcomes; for example, for seventh grade, an average of 50 students needed remediation after planned instruction (in all three teachers' classes: Alex, Ania, and Roland). However, Alex had less than 15% of MLs needing remediation in his classes, while other teachers were closer to 60%.

These initial achievement outcomes for MLs, as reported by three out of the five science teachers, were significant in that they demonstrated that the intentional planning and application of the equity-driven PLC and its components they co-created were yielding some positive outcomes for MLs.

(Re)framing the PLC Work

(Re)framing the PLC work to become more equitable for and about MLs impacts all levels: district, school, and classroom. The (re)framed PLC work requires (1) a shift in culture from high-stakes and top-down accountability to structures that are grounded on equity and allow authentic collaboration, inquiry, reflection, teacher agency, and deep learning models for teachers to develop professionally; (2) a shift from rigid schedules "covering" curriculum to creating the right conditions of adequate time and spaces for deep learning for teachers and students; and (3) a shift from "one-size-fits-all" types of instructional approaches to practices that are informed by who students are culturally and linguistically.

NOTES

1. *Multilingual learner* is a term that has often been used in English as a second language, foreign language learning, and applied linguistics literature (Garcia & Sylvan, 2011; Henry, 2017; Jessner et al., 2016; Kramsch & Gerhards, 2012; Van Sluys & Rao, 2012). The term *multilingual learner* denotes a holistic approach to the child as a learner of multiple languages in multilingual environments within the U.S. context.

2. Professional learning communities (PLCs), in theory, provide the ongoing means for teachers to plan instruction, collaborate, reflect, and adjust practices to improve student learning (DuFour et al., 2010; Hargreaves & Fullan, 2012; Hord, 2008).

3. *Binds* represent the barriers created by the power within the discourses of whiteness shaping the district's PLCs and the science teachers' pedagogical practices.

4. *Unravels* represent the ways the science teachers disrupted whiteness by resisting or eliminating the negative influences impacting MLs in science education.

5. Names of all districts, schools, and teachers referred to in this chapter are pseudonyms.

6. The PLC Results Cycle Framework is the framework adopted by Las Colinas School District to inform how grade-level or content-area teams engage with a standard-based instructional cycle. The PLC Results Cycle's purpose is to provide the conditions of time and space for teachers to plan collaboratively for the content, the pedagogical approaches for delivering instruction, and the assessments to assess learning.

7. Discourses of whiteness can be unpacked as (1) privileged access to tangible goods, whose mechanisms are maintained through the notions of meritocracy and entitlement (DiAngelo, 2011); (2) niceness, whose mechanisms are incoherence, fragility, and ignorance (Bonilla-Silva, 2015; DiAngelo, 2011; Levine-Rasky, 2000); and (3) evasiveness, whose mechanisms are colorblindness, color muteness, coded language, defensiveness, and avoidance to critique (Bonilla-Silva, 2015; Castagno, 2008; DiAngelo, 2011; Frankenberg, 1993; Giroux, 1997; Haviland, 2008; Leonardo, 2007; Levine-Rasky, 2000; Marx, 2006; Thompson, 2003).

8. *Tier II instruction* or *small-group instruction* in a multi-tier system of support refers to instruction for students that did not meet the standard of instruction (usually about 15% of the student population) in a Tier I setting.

9. *Tier I instruction* or *whole-group instruction* in a multi-tier system of supports refers to instruction accessible and achievable by at least 80% of the student population.

10. *CREDE* refers to a set of culturally and linguistically informed standards developed by the Center for Research on Education, Diversity & Excellence.

11. The 5Es Framework refers to *engage, explore, explain, evaluate*, and *extend* and language development in science education (Beltran et al., 2013).

12. The 6Cs Framework refers to *critical thinking, collaboration, communication, creativity, character*, and *citizenship* and is also known as 21st-century skills (Bunch & Walqui, 2019; Fullan et al., 2018).

13. Layering means a process in which teachers study, pose questions, critically analyze, and find connections between the district's existing frameworks and then unpack the connecting elements for the knowledge, language, dispositions, and skills teachers and students need in order to make science education equitable for all students, and especially for MLs.

14. Teachers become activators as well as facilitators of knowledge so students have additional opportunities to clarify or correct misconceptions, fill information gaps, attach academic language to student-friendly language and use it in context, and engage students in metacognitive strategies.

15. Collaborative inquiry is thus a powerful and practical form of capacity building that gives adults a deep-learning model and experience that mirrors what we are hoping they will do with students (Fullan et al., 2018, p. 101).

REFERENCES

Alim, H. S., & Paris, D. (2017). What is culturally sustaining pedagogy and why does it matter? In H. S. Alim & D. Paris (Eds.), *Culturally sustaining pedagogies: Teaching and learning for justice in a changing world* (pp. 1–21). Teachers College Press.

Beltran, D., Sarmiento, L., & Mora-Flores, E. (2013). Managing and maximizing language development through inquiry-based science. In *Science for English Language Learners* (pp. 9–44). Shell Educational Publishing.

Bonilla-Silva, E. (2015). The structure of racism in color-blind, "post-racial" America. *American Behavioral Scientist, 59*(11), 1358–1376. SAGE.

Bunch, G., & Walqui, A. (2019). Educating English learners in the 21st century. In A. Walqui & G. C. Bunch (Eds.), *Amplifying the curriculum: Designing quality learning opportunities for English learners* (pp. 1–16). Teachers College Press.

Castagno, A. (2008). "I don't want to hear that!": Legitimating whiteness through silence in schools. *Anthropology & Education Quarterly, 39*(3), pp. 314–333. DOI:10.1111/j.1548-1492.2008.00024.x.

DiAngelo, R. (2011). White fragility. *International Journal of Critical Pedagogy, 3*(3), 54–70.

DuFour, R., DuFour, R., Eaker, R., & Many, T. (2010). *Learning by doing: A handbook for professional learning communities at work* (2nd ed.). Solution Tree Press.

Frankenberg, R. (1993). White women, race matters: The social construction of whiteness. In R. Delgado & J. Stefancic (Eds.), *Critical White studies: Looking behind the mirror* (pp. 632–634). Temple University Press.

Fullan, M., Quinn, J., & McEachen, J. (2018). *Deep learning: Engage the world change the world.* Corwin.

Garcia, O., & Sylvan, C. E. (2011). Pedagogies and practices in multilingual classrooms: Singularities in pluralities. *The Modern Language Journal, 95*(iii), 385–400. doi: 10.1111/j.1540-4781.2011.01208.x

Giroux, H. A. (1997). Rewriting the discourse of racial identity: Towards a pedagogy and politics of Whiteness. *Harvard Educational Review, 67*(2), 285–320.

Hargreaves, A., & Fullan, M (2012). *Professional capital: Transforming teaching in every school.* Teachers College Press, Columbia University.

Haviland, V. S. (2008). "Things get glossed over": Rearticulating the silencing power of whiteness in education. *Journal of Teacher Education, 59*(1), 40–54. doi: 10.1177/0022487107310751.

Henry, A. (2017). L2 motivation and multilingual identities. *The Modern Language Journal, 101*(3), 548–565. doi: 10.1111/modl.12412 0026–7902/17/548–565.

Hord, S. M. (2008). Evolution of the professional learning community: Revolutionary concept is based on intentional collegial learning. *Journal of Staff Development, 29*(3), 10–13.

Jessner, U., Allgäuer-Hackl, E., & Hofer, B. (2016). Emerging multilingual awareness in educational contexts: From theory to practice. *The Canadian Modern Language Review/La Revue canadienne des langues vivantes, 72*(2), 157–182. doi:10.3138/cmlr.2746

Kramsch, C., & Gerhards, S. (2012). Im Gespräch: An interview with Claire Kramsch on the "multilingual subject." *Die Unterrichtspraxis/Teaching German, 45*(1), 74–82.

Leonardo, Z. (2007). The war on schools: NCLB, nation creation and the educational construction of whiteness. *Race Ethnicity and Education, 10*(3), 261–278. doi: 10.1080/13613320701503249

Levine-Rasky, C. (2000). Framing whiteness: Working through the tensions in introducing whiteness to educators. *Race Ethnicity and Education, 3*(3), 271–292. doi: 10.1080/713693039

Marx, S. (2006). *Revealing the invisible: Confronting passive racism in teacher education.* Routledge, Taylor & Francis Group.

Patel, L. (2016). *Decolonizing educational research: From ownership to answerability.* Routledge.

Thompson, A. (2003). Tiffany, friend of people of color: White investments in antiracism. *Qualitative Studies in Education, 16*(1), 7–29.

Van Sluys, K., & Rao, A. (2012). Supporting multilingual learners: Practical theory and theoretical practices. *Theory Into Practice, 51*, 281–289. doi: 10.1080/00405841.2012.726056

About the Editors and Contributors

Antonette Aragon, Ph.D., is an associate professor in Colorado State University's School of Education and a race scholar in the Race and Intersectional Studies for Educational Equity (RISE) program.

H. Prentice Baptiste, Ph.D., is a Regents and Distinguished Achievement Professor, and in 2014 was awarded the first College of Education Diversity Award at New Mexico State University. He was president (2016 to 2018) of the National Association for Multicultural Education (NAME), a premier organization advocating for equity and social justice, which he helped found in 1990. His research interests include the conceptualization of multicultural education, the process of multiculturalizing educational entities, and culturally diversifying science and mathematics instruction. Baptiste has authored or edited seven books, as well as more than 140 articles, papers, and chapters on multicultural and science education He has presented papers and conducted workshops in Nigeria, Egypt, Germany, Jamaica, Kenya, Morocco, and the Netherlands. As President of NAME, he was co-leader of two educational cultural groups to Cuba.

Judith Blakely, Ph.D., is an educational specialist. She is certified in multiple states as a school superintendent, school administrator (pre-K–12 principal), and director of special, bilingual, and gifted education. She is also a member of the National Association for Bilingual Education (providing work and service to the discipline of world language). Blakely presently serves in the role of Academic Coordinator at Walden University and works to serve a vital role in maximizing student achievement by incorporating leadership, advocacy, and collaboration. She believes in team effort and works tirelessly to promote equity and access to opportunities and rigorous educational experiences for all students. Blakely's motto is: "Together we can!" Raised in Chicago by her mother and father, a Chicago Public School teacher and a small business owner respectively, she developed a passion early for education and service. To this end, she co-founded an educational social service agency that advocates for underrepresented members of society through personal development, education, and social service programs. With offerings such as advocacy for the special needs community, tutoring, resume writing, goal setting workshops, parenting workshops, literacy training, student workshops, and teacher classroom assistance, Blakely empowers individuals and communities to break the cycle of underachievement and create legacies of success. She believes that education is the door to opportunity and living a life of abundance, and that this is a gift that should be afforded to all.

Analis Carattini-Ruiz is an educator with 20 years of experience. She has spent the last 12 years as an administrator overseeing both federal and state programs for students learning English as a new language.

Cliff Chestnutt, Ph.D., is an assistant professor in the Department of Early Childhood through Secondary Education.

Kevin Donley is a doctoral candidate in critical and sociocultural studies in education at the University of Oregon.

Ashraf Esmail, Ph.D., is an associate professor and program coordinator of criminal justice at Dillard University. He is the Director for the Center for Racial Justice and Barron Hilton Criminal Justice Endowed Professor. His areas of research include race and social justice, multicultural, urban, and peace education. He is on the boards for the National Association for Multicultural Education, National Association for Peace Education, World Association for Academic Doctors, and Court Watch Nola.

Jan Perry Evenstad, Ph.D., is executive director of the Western Educational Equity Assistance Center at Metropolitan State University of Denver, one of four regional centers funded by the U.S. Department of Education providing technical assistance on civil rights in K–12 education.

Georgina Y. García, Ed.D., is currently a principal analyst specializing in educational equity and advocacy for multilingual learners of English, teacher learning, and classroom practices at the Western Educational Equity Assistance Center (WEEAC) at Metropolitan State University of Denver.

Holly D. Glaser, Ph.D., is an adjunct faculty member in the College of Education and Human Development at George Mason University, where she teaches undergraduate- and graduate-level courses in gifted education and elementary education.

Rubén A. González is a Ph.D. student in race, inequality, and language in education at Stanford University.

Kathleen M. Hargiss is the former associate dean of academics and chair for the Graduate School of Business (MBA) at Florida Metropolitan University.

Immaculée Harushimana is a 2018–2019 Fulbright Scholar (Mzuzu University, Mw) and associate professor of TESOL and English education at Lehman College, City University of New York.

Courtney A. Howard, Ph.D., is associate professor of education, a center director, and an associate dean at the College of Charleston.

Nan Li is a professor of education at Claflin University and an active members of the CAEP site team. She has authored 28 publications and served as president of the South Carolina Association for Teacher Educators.

Hsiao-Ching Lin is an instructor and a Ph.D. candidate in the School of Education at Colorado State University (CSU).

Kristin Kline Liu is a senior research associate at the NCEO and the principal investigator of the Improving Instruction for English Learners Through Improved Accessibility Decisions project.

Alice Duhon-Ross McCallum, Ph.D., is a core faculty for the Richard W. Riley College of Education at Walden University. Her current research focus is multicultural, international, peace education. She is a career educator with over thirty years of teaching in higher education and is a Nationally Board-Certified Counselor and National Board-Certified School Counselor. She is the past Region 5 Regional Director for the National Association for Multicultural Education Advancing and Avocation for Social Justice & Equity and serves on several advisory and editorial boards.

Michele L. McConnell has 22 years of combined experience in teaching English and English as a second language in high school and community colleges, community college reading courses, and teacher education courses at a four-year university.

Erica C. Meadows is a Ph.D. candidate and adjunct faculty member in the College of Education and Human Development at George Mason University.

Charity Funfe Tatah Mentan, Ph.D., is a research associate with the National Center for Educational Outcomes (NCEO) who specializes in the development of culturally and linguistically diverse resources for inclusive communities.

Kelly Metz-Matthews teaches in and coordinates the WRITE program at the University of San Diego, where she also serves as affiliate faculty in the Liberal Studies Department.

Leah M. Mortenson is a clinical instructor at St. John's University in Queens, New York, working with preservice K–12 teachers, and she also teaches part-time in English for Academic Purposes programs at various universities around New York.

Kym O'Donnell is a graduate research assistant with the Improving Instruction for English Learners Through Improved Accessibility Decisions project at NCEO, while working on a Ph.D. in second language education.

Judith A. Orth, Ph.D., is a pedagogical professional with over 50 years of experience in public and higher education.

David Parker, Ph.D., is a university educator, consultant, motivational artist, and author of books for children.

Darrell Peterson is an education program specialist at NCEO and is the project coordinator for the Improving Instruction for English Learners Through Improved Accessibility Decisions project.

Abul Pitre, Ph.D., is professor and department chair of Africana Studies at San Francisco State University. He was appointed Edinboro University's first named professor for his outstanding work in African American education and held the distinguished title of Carter G. Woodson Professor of Education.

Renee Shank is a lecturer at the College of Education, University of Washington–Seattle.

Andrea Smith, Ph.D., is an assistant professor at the University of West Georgia in the Department of Early Childhood Through Secondary Education.

Erin Smith is an assistant professor in the School of Education at the University of Southern Mississippi in Hattiesburg, Mississippi.

Glori Hodge Smith received her undergraduate degree in history teaching, master's degree in media literacy education, and doctorate in curriculum and instruction.

Camacia Smith-Ross, Ed.D., is a tenured professor at Southern University and A&M College, the only Historically Black College and University System in the country. She is a former Vice-Provost for Academic Affairs and serves as the current Executive Director for Pre-College and Outreach Programs. Dr. Smith-Ross has a combined 27 years in K–12 and higher education. She has been recognized for her commitment with working with first generational, minority students. Dr. Smith-Ross is an avid researcher and accomplished publisher.

Verónica E. Valdez is an associate professor in the Department of Education, Culture, and Society at the University of Utah.

Lin Wu is an assistant professor at the College of Education, Western Oregon University.

Yi-Chen Wu is a research associate at the National Center on Educational Outcomes in Minneapolis, Minnesota.

Nuo Xu is a Ph.D. candidate in the Department of Education, Culture, and Society at the University of Utah.

www.ingramcontent.com/pod-product-compliance
Lightning Source LLC
Chambersburg PA
CBHW031710230426
43668CB00006B/175